MEDIATION: THE BOOK

A Step-by-Step Guide
for
Dispute Resolvers

Sam Leonard

EVANSTON PUBLISHING, INC.
EVANSTON, ILLINOIS 60201

EVANSTON PUBLISHING, INC.
1571 SHERMAN AVE., ANNEX C
EVANSTON, ILLINOIS 60201

Printed in the U.S.A.

10 9 8 7 6 5 4

ISBN: 1-879260-25-5

Illustrations by Lisa Hamburg

ABOUT THE AUTHOR

Dispute resolution specialist and paradigm pioneer Sam Leonard, B.A., M.Div., is the executive director of the Institute for Mediation & Arbitration Training, a national dispute training academy headquartered in Denver, Colorado, and Palm Springs, California. He also is the founder/president of the Center for Solutions, a private dispute resolution firm, located in Denver, and serves on the faculty of the University of Denver Graduate School in its University College dispute resolution program.

For the past 15 years, Leonard has conducted more than 1,200 mediations, arbitrations and consultations with families, government agencies, religious bodies, private corporations, hospitals and other clients. He is affiliated with the Alban Institute of Washington, D.C., the Academy of Family Mediators, Association of Family and Conciliation Courts, the Society for Professionals in Dispute Resolution, the American Bar Association Section on Alternative Dispute Resolution (ADR) and the American Arbitration Association, for which he serves on its national mediation panel.

The Center and Institute offer training for mediators, where Leonard has trained hundreds of students using the techniques he has developed. The father of modern mediation, John Haynes, attended a seminar taught by Leonard and said, "This workshop was the best I have ever attended at any conference. His method was a superb training technique that enabled people to grasp concepts quickly."

Leonard was honored by the Denver Bar Association and the Denver Judges for training attorneys and judges to prepare for "Settlement Week" — one week set aside in the courts in 1989 where more than 600 civil cases were settled, and again in 1990, where more than 650 reached settlement, using mediation. This prototype has become a model for other judicial districts across the United States.

The Center for Solutions was listed as one of the top fifty dispute resolution firms in 1992 by Faulkner and Grey in terms of caseload.

Educational projects spearheaded by the author include a mediator/attorney ADR seminar in conjunction with the Denver Bar Association; an organizational dispute resolution training course in Albuquerque, New Mexico; a two-time training program for Denver Settlement Week; the University of Alabama School of Law; the San Luis Valley Mediation Project; the Boulder Peace Institute; and an international education program for the Lutheran Church.

Leonard has been featured in numerous print, radio and television interviews, and has published several articles on alternative dispute resolution. He is a member of the International Speaker's Network and Who's Who Registry of Global Business Leaders.

One recent student of Sam Leonard wrote: "Six stars plus! ...the strongest course I have ever taken."

ACKNOWLEDGMENTS AND DEDICATION

Writing a book is tough work. Without the support and inspiration I have received from many people, this book would still only be a concept.

Special thanks to:

Jane Humphries, my wonderful writing consultant.

Lisa Hamburg, who created the unique illustrations.

My clients, who have taught me more than I have taught them.

This book is dedicated to:

Adam, the kid who calls me "Dad" and continually reminds me how to dream.

Katherine, who has shared the dream for many years and lives it out every single day.

And Paul, who believes in the dreamer.

INTRODUCTION

The American judicial process is in serious trouble, a morass of delays and expensive litigation. Small disputes take a year or more to resolve, costing all concerned parties wasted dollars and hours.

The time has come for the mediator to step on the stage. We have entered a new shift of values, a new paradigm, from the old "I'll see you in court" legacy to a roundtable technique where disputants lay their problems on the table and come to a resolution, with the help of a coach on the sidelines — the mediator.

This process saves disputants, courts and taxpayers untold millions of dollars, freeing the court calendars for cases that require jury trials. Everyone benefits.

Mediation is the profession of the 1990s and the 21st Century. The excesses of the 1980s, the superfluous spending in private and public sectors, the savings and loans scandals, the inflated credit card purchases, have swung the pendulum to the lean side as we enter the mid-decade of the '90s. Top-heavy corporations are tightening their belts and laying off workers. Consumers are weary of buying expensive, inferior goods. Many businesses have folded.

A positive shift of priorities is now taking place. Care for the planet's welfare is rising. People are searching for meaning in their lives instead of showing off their BMWs and Cadillacs. Spree spending has given way to the quest for quality products and services. Those of real value will last. The rest will fall by the wayside.

Mediation is the new profession for the mental health professional who wants to move in a new direction, or for that bright individual who has much to contribute but no longer wants to work as an attorney. Or, for the real estate broker leaving a sluggish market, or for the MBA in that large corporation that made too many widgets for people to buy every year. Mediation is for dedicated, gutsy pioneers who see the vista of change and growth. Mediation is for entrepreneurs. Mediation is for men and women with a vision.

Are you qualified to be a mediator? You will know much more when you have finished this book. No punches are pulled. *Mediation: The Book* will let you know if you have "the stuff" to enter the alternative dispute resolution field, and will show you how to go about it.

Remember the words of Federico Fellini as you read this book: "The visionary is the only true realist."

— Sam Leonard

CONTENTS

PART ONE

Of Conflicts, Disputes and Other Creatures from the Black Lagoon

The Creature

ONE

Genesis: A Personal Story

It was an idyllic summer afternoon on the outskirts of Greensboro, North Carolina — hot, sultry, a perfect kid's day. Randy and I were playing in the woods. We were both six years old and the best friends on earth. I remember the tall pine trees and the sun glistening through the needles. We were building a tree house.

Even then, I was a take-charge guy. Randy and I found ourselves in an argument over the construction of this tree house. I wanted to build walls to make it secure, so we could sleep at night and not fall out, or play war games and not have an accident.

Randy did not want walls on the tree house. I never found out why. "He is so lazy," I thought. "I am the only one who works around here anyway."

I was determined that we were going to put walls on that tree house. Randy was just as adamant that no walls would be built. We exchanged words:

"We will build the walls."

"We will not build the walls."

One verbal volley evoked another. The altercation soon escalated into a physical fight, screaming and wrestling and rolling on the ground. I was two inches shorter than Randy, which was nothing new. I was always shorter than everybody else. It did not matter: the battle was on. I was determined not to lose.

Randy's father heard us and came on the scene. He told Randy that if he lost that fight, he would be punished. Randy's father was a big man, an ex-military guy, about 8'3" (from the viewpoint of a six year old). He was mean and gruff, standing there barking out orders.

"Randy! If you don't beat him up, I will whip your hide when you get home."

The fight continued. As with all fights, it seemed to go on forever. I was caught up in winning. I twisted his arm behind his back and rubbed his face into the ground. I beat the tar out of this kid. That ended the fight.

Randy went home crying. I have no idea what happened between him and his father.

Afterwards, I felt miserable. I had lost my best friend and the dream of the tree house. A couple of years later Randy's little brother died of leukemia. I remember feeling bad. But Randy and I were not friends anymore, so I did nothing.

Over the years Randy and I periodically talked to each other but our friendship was broken forever. The tree house was never finished — just a few boards rotting in the breeze.

My fight with Randy and the pain it brought were probably instrumental in my decision to enter the field of conflict resolution many years later. That memory reminds me that there must be a better way to settle disputes.

HISTORIC WAYS OF SETTLING DISPUTES

To honor that experience, I keep a file of scenes which underscores the stupidity of violence, entitled "Historic Ways of Settling Disputes."

One picture shows a man struck down by his rival's bullet in a traditional duel with pistols. Another scene portrays a swordsman piercing a lesser-talented foe through the heart in a duel to the death. A third offers the spectacle of two men going full blast, with their fists in the air, a popular form of dispute resolution within male-dominated cultures.

A fourth visual shows people fighting with double six-shooters in the Old West. Several men on each side of the conflict come out of buildings, with guns blazing, raising smoke and dust.

A fifth image depicts conflict in a courtroom setting. A judge in the background presides over the courtroom. In the foreground are two attorneys squaring off, pointing at each other in blaming, accusatory postures. They are hired guns, defending their clients who are seated behind them.

Another image represents the ultimate resolution of conflict — war. It shows a small town being attacked from the sky. Bombs explode on the ground, with fire engulfing people and buildings. My file folder is now bursting with examples. As Kurt Vonnegut wrote: "And so it goes..."

We do not need to draw pistols on each other or to engage in epée duels at sunrise or have gunfights at the OK Corral. Nothing is written that demands that we spill blood in courtrooms or drop bombs on our enemies. *A better way exists to resolve our disputes. That better way is mediation.*

This book is based on the following values:
- That conflict is inevitable and is all around us.
- That how we handle conflict determines whether it is healthy or unhealthy, constructive or destructive.
- That disputes belong foremost to the persons engaged in the conflict not to courts or attorneys or systems.
- That virtually every human being in a dispute wants to settle it.
- That relationships are more important than disputes.
- That a win/win solution is preferable to a win/lose or lose/lose outcome.
- That individuals in conflict are the best crafters of a settlement which works for them.
- That disputants always have choices to make.
- That the wounds each of us has received from conflicts make us wise by linking us to the brokenness of others in a dispute. As Chief Seattle said, "All things are connected, like the blood which unites one family."

- That it is imperative to deal with both "head" and "heart" in effective dispute resolution.
- That mediation is hard work and is integral in creating a better world.

This book will:
- Build a foundation for understanding conflict.
- Offer tools for diagnosing conflict.
- Present the perspective that a vast paradigm shift is occurring.
- Give an understanding of mediation as a dispute resolution mechanism.
- Take a look at the personhood of the mediator.
- Consider the nuts and bolts of mediation.
- Extend to the reader a step-by-step system of mediation.
- Suggest tips for setting up a mediation practice.
- Create a philosophical and ethical context out of which to work.

Mediation has both a technology and a magic to it. Recently I hiked near my log cabin in the Colorado Rockies. Snow-capped peaks. Crystal clear streams. Aspen trees. Birds. Chipmunks. A multitude of mountain flowers in fireworks bloom.

I stumbled across an artist who was gazing at the same magnificent scene. Moving closer, I beheld a beautiful interpretation in oils of that which we both saw with our eyes.

I could enroll in art classes for the next 50 years and learn the *techniques* of painting. But I could never create the *art*. (Trust me on this one. The only "D" I ever made was in art class!)

This book will share the techniques of mediation. The art is left up to you.

TWO

Conflict on the Third Planet from the Sun

HIGH DRAMA VIGNETTES OF DESTRUCTIVE CONFLICT

If you look around in your everyday life, read a newspaper, watch the news or go to a church or synagogue, you will encounter conflict. Take, for example, the case of the organist and the minister in a small church on the east coast. They bickered constantly over the type of music to be played, the quality of the music, and how the hymns should blend with the service to make it whole. The conflict escalated. Finally, one Sunday morning the organist was about to play at the morning service. Her hands hit the keys of the organ for the first rousing chord. Her fingers would not budge...the keyboard was covered with Super Glue.

Destructive conflict is everywhere, even in your favorite place of worship.

A friend was playing mixed doubles on the public tennis court one Sunday morning. She was about to serve when she noticed all activity had stopped on the adjoining courts. Two courts to the right she saw a strange sight: two grown men lying on the court, flaying at

Conflict on the Third Planet from the Sun

each other. Later, she learned they had disagreed over the score.

Destructive conflict happens in places where one least expects it.

A 1993 trade union dispute set off a bizarre reaction in the State of Kerala in southern India. An angry mob was so enraged that they broke into a zoo near the town of Kannur and attacked more than 100 rare snakes, as well as other birds and animals. They poured kerosene on 30 animal cages, setting them on fire. The victims included six porcupines, seven turtles, 30 white rats, 30 rabbits, two peacocks, six migratory birds, two vultures, an eagle and a king cobra which was first beaten to death.

Destructive conflict is everywhere, and the innocent suffer.

A Maryland attorney was disbarred for breaking into a house and killing a kitten in a microwave oven. The attorney and a friend, both drunk, had been trespassing in the home of the estranged wife of a former client, hunting for stock certificates. Max, the woman's seven-month-old kitten, scampered underfoot. This irritated the attorney to no end. He put Max in the microwave oven. The attorney "accidentally" leaned against the wrong button of the microwave, and that was the end of Max.

Destructive conflict hurts all creatures who get in the way.

A wealthy divorcing couple had resolved all their issues except one: who would receive custody of Ralph the Rottweiler? They feuded, pouring thousands of dollars into the pockets of their divorce attorneys. One evening the man, returning from work, pulled into his driveway. Sitting on his front porch, eyes wide open, was Ralph the Rottweiler. The man knew that he had won this final battle. He walked over to the dog and reached out to stroke him...but Ralph did not move. Our man had won the battle but not the war. The dog had been stuffed by his ex-wife's taxidermist.

Destructive conflict is often absurd.

Then there is the story of the 55-year-old real estate investor who was "out to get the lawyers" who represented his opponent in a lawsuit. He walked into their San Francisco law firm, packing three handguns, and started shooting. He got his revenge, all right. He killed eight people and wounded six others, before killing himself.

Destructive conflict brings out the lowest common denominator in people.

In November 1992 the State of Colorado passed Amendment 2 which nullified local anti-discrimination laws to protect gays and lesbians. The amendment had been sponsored by a coalition of conservative right-wing Christians. In essence, it was designed to allow discrimination against homosexuals. As the controversy reached a peak, the citizens of Colorado found themselves split into two highly conflicted camps.

The conflict brought problems to the school systems, the workplace, housing, and other areas where human rights could be violated. The negative publicity also hurt the economy. The Colorado Bar Association struggled over whether or not to hold its annual convention in Colorado Springs, where it had met for the past 71 years, because the mayor had allegedly referred to homosexuals as "queers." The loss of revenue estimated to the State of Colorado may reach into the multi-millions of dollars. Relationships have been damaged. The very social fabric of the state as a community has been torn.

The backlash of that conflict was evident in speeches made by members of the neo-Nazis and the Ku Klux Klan during the 1993 Martin Luther King Day in Denver. Normally these hate groups direct their energy against Jews and African-Americans. This year the rhetoric was aimed towards homosexuals. "Faggots are maggots," was a favorite epithet.

Destructive conflict often polarizes.

During the summer of 1993, a wife severed her husband's penis in retaliation for his allegedly raping her. Apparently, she fled the house with the penis and threw it out the window of her car. The organ was found in a field and reattached to the man.

Destructive conflict often brings about the loss of our most valuable things!

A CONFLICTED ENVIRONMENT CALLED LIFE

It is common for people to say to me, "Sam, we don't have any conflict in our lives. Conflict is about other people. It is what we read about in the newspapers, what we see on television, what we hear on the radio. Conflict is about dramatic situations that do not happen to us." On one of my days off, I took a pad of paper with me and counted every conflict situation I encountered in my everyday life. I tallied 128.

- On the freeway a man in the fast lane cut in front of a woman in the next lane, forcing her to stand on her brakes, as he raced across all four lanes to reach his exit. The elegant, well-dressed woman gave him the finger.
- In the grocery check-out line, a woman was in front of me with her freckle-faced four-year-old boy who was trying to grab a candy bar (displayed at child eye level). The woman DRAGGED him through the line, scolding him all the while: "NO! You can't have that! You're going to spoil your dinner!"
- While strolling through the mall, I saw a young couple emerge from a jewelry store. They were arguing vehemently over which wedding ring to buy. He: "It's too expensive. We're not going to waste money that way." She: "This is the most important event in my life. I want everything to be perfect."
- As I sat enjoying a quiet lunch in an expensive restaurant, I heard angry voices wafting from behind the kitchen door, disturbing the soft music, white tablecloths, fresh flowers and fine cuisine. The manager was chewing out a waiter. This verbal altercation took place at the height of the business lunch hour. There was a loud crash of dishes. The waiter stormed out of the restaurant.

Now when people tell me there is no conflict around them, I view them as either pickled, oblivious or dead!

Although people may not realize it, life is a series of conflicts.

THE CREATURE FROM THE BLACK LAGOON

As a child in the 1950s I watched again and again a movie called *The Creature from the Black Lagoon,* a grade B horror flick. At auspicious moments in the plot, a horrible, scaly monster dripping with black ooze would emerge from the swamp, the boiling water gurgling and bubbling, the fog swirling around the bog. With gills flapping, this hideous creature would suddenly appear and steal the girl. Sometimes it would attack the hero at night. I loved this film. Today it is a classic.

Most people in our culture shun conflict, viewing it as a fearsome force which surfaces from the unknown. Conflict is the Alien, the Bogeyman. It is bigger than life, mean, harsh, dark and foreboding. It raises its hideous head at the most inopportune moments and it grabs you!

You never have a chance. You cannot see or smell or hear it. It attacks you at moments least expected. You are in the icy death-grip of conflict.

THREE

Defining Conflict

From childhood on, most people in America are raised to believe that conflict does not exist. This is *conflict denial.* Coupled with this inherent blind spot of denial is the fear of conflict. Conflict is the unknown, the monster of our deepest terrors. And people try to run away from it at all costs. This is *conflict avoidance.*

Most people see conflict as bigger than life, ugly beyond their worst nightmares. Conflict is dark and evil. We perceive that conflict, by its very nature, wrecks marriages, destroys relationships, hurts business, and interferes with life. Thus, we choose to avoid conflict in our lives. Surely we will perish if we engage in conflict. To deny conflict or to avoid it seems much safer. But is it?

GROWING UP IN DIFFERENT PARTS OF THE UNITED STATES

New England: A friend shared with me how conflict was handled in her home. The old Victorian maxim, "Children are meant to be seen, not heard," lingered on in New England families. If children did speak, they had to do so intelligently on broad subjects they learned in school. The young were to be molded and crammed with

Conflict — Dark and Evil

topics animal, vegetable and mineral. Scholarship, self-discipline and the performance of one's duty were virtues. Authority was never questioned.

Children were taught not to express their feelings. Adults did not show their children communication skills to work through conflicts. When asked, "How are you?" the expected response was a variation on the non-statement, "I am fine." This was the norm even in the midst of seething conflict.

The Midwest: A colleague shared her memories of how conflict was handled in her middle class WASP home. As in New England, conflict was to be denied, avoided and closeted. Everyone in the family knew it was bad and that it was somebody's fault, so they made sure it was not their fault.

If you were angry with your sibling, it was acceptable to be outspoken to the point of insensitivity and rudeness. Actual physical violence was rare. Minor physical violence — hitting and slapping — was part of growing up. You did it in secret so your parents could not see what was happening. Of course, parents often knew what was going on and occasionally had to intervene, using some physical force.

Blaming others was the primary method of dealing with interpersonal conflicts within the family. No one needed to pretend by exchanging pleasantries with others in the immediate family.

Outside the family, you pointed fingers but never confronted the "guilty" party. You sought out others, talked about the other party and aligned your allies, developing an armed camp of supporters. If the other party confronted you directly (which rarely happened in the Midwest), you denied there was a problem.

Admitting one's own fault, acknowledging responsibility, was never an option. Crying, yelling or showing any other real feelings was unacceptable. You put on a face for the outside world so no one would have a clue as to what was going on.

The conflict would be left to smolder and fester, undermining relationships. Friends would stop speaking to each other. Sometimes the involved parties and their allies would not speak to each other for a while, and then one day the dispute would be dropped, without anyone discussing the problems, without acknowledging even that tproblems existed, or attempting resolution. One of the involved parties would take the initiative, and suddenly the parties would be speaking to each other. The disagreement would never be talked about. No apologies or gestures of forgiveness would occur.

The South: I grew up in the genteel South. The primary value imprinted on us was to be "nice" to one another. If anything disrupted the niceties, it was wrong. People of my childhood world were divided into two parts: the Nice and the Not-Nice. If my parents raised their voices in my presence, the appearance of propriety was damaged; and this was unsatisfactory. I remember family members having strong underlying conflicts with each other. These conflicts were kept under the surface or people were talked about behind their backs. All conflict was perceived as disruptive to the core value of "niceness."

In my Southern world, the Civil Rights Movement of the 1960s opened a Pandora's Box of conflict. On the surface, all was well. White people were happy with the status quo. Then the Creature from the Black Lagoon emerged — and massive conflict in the South erupted over civil rights issues between the black and white communities. As a teenager, I lived in the middle of it, and that struggle became a crucial part of who I am today.

The West: I interviewed a 95-year-old man who grew up in the western part of the U.S. This man was a salty character and I learned much from him. I asked him how people settled their differences when they were serious. He paused, thought for a moment and said, "First they'd be spoken to...then hit...then shot." Maybe growing up in the South wasn't so bad!

Recently I came across a newspaper article by Miss Manners entitled, "Carrying On a Feud with Decorum." For etiquette's sake, she advises that people show consideration to each other, no matter how despicable any of the parties may be. If someone offends another, apologies are forthcoming, followed by gracious thanks.

But what to do if the offendee is beyond redemption, beyond the pale of civilization? We cannot easily get rid of the person unless we wish to go to jail for murder. Miss Manners suggests that we steer a wide berth around the unfortunate being. If by chance you accidentally meet, you employ the art of "cutting, " i.e. pretending you do not see one another.

We must not engage in nasty talk about our enemy, says Miss Manners. But if we simply cannot resist, apply the saccharine of

Pandora's Box of Conflict

sympathy: "I feel so sorry for him — he really isn't himself any more."

With the exception perhaps of the old man from the West, it appears that many of us were brought up to deny and avoid conflict — and this is perpetuated today by the likes of Miss Manners. But what is conflict? Let's take a look.

HEITLER'S DEFINITION

Conflict is not a negative, dark, ugly force whose essence is, by definition, always destructive. In 1991 Susan Heitler wrote a landmark book, *From Conflict to Resolution.*[1] It is the first book in the dispute resolution literature that addresses intra-personal conflict and emotional disorders that are internal to the individual, and then moves to inter-personal conflict, community conflict and global conflict.

In her book, Heitler wrote: "Conflict involves a situation in which *seemingly* incompatible elements exert force in opposing or divergent directions." In reality, this may not be so, although the affected parties believe otherwise.

We need to examine opposing and divergent conflicts. An opposing conflict is described as such: Two neighbors have lived side by side for 28 years. Jane Doe, who is elderly, has acquired a Doberman pinscher to protect herself after the death of her husband, Harry Doe. Helen Smith, also an elderly widow, has difficulty sleeping.

Helen's perspective: "That stupid Doberman pinscher barks at the drop of a pin all night long." *Helen wants the dog to stop barking.* In Jane Doe's mind-set: "I spent hard-earned money to purchase a trained watchdog." *She expects her dog to be free to respond to any noise or threat.* Jane's and Helen's goals are seemingly incompatible, two spears pointed at each other in deadlock.

The next example presents a divergent conflict. Recently I was brought into a large beverage manufacturing corporation. I was working with employees in the company's human resources department who were in conflict over diverse positions on affirmative action policies. The conflict had escalated to a level where all eight individuals in the department were in adversarial relationships, all going in eight different directions. There was no common vision. In addition, the department goals had not been clearly defined. It was a mess. This "going in different directions" produced conflict.

Heitler defines conflict:

>...*a situation in which seemingly incompatible elements exert force in opposing or divergent directions.* These divergent forces evoke tension, but not necessarily hostility or fighting....the word conflict does not necessarily connote argument or battle. Conflicts may be silent and unexpressed. Individuals who avoid speaking to one another, or who refrain from discussion of sensitive issues, may be manifesting signs of conflict. The term conflict denotes only that elements appear to be in opposition.[2]

LEONARD'S DEFINITION

From my perspective, *conflict* is a dynamic in which concerns, needs, interests or positions are opposed to one another either by perception or in reality. A *dispute* is a crystallized conflict problem which offers the possibility of a settlement.

To unpack these definitions, note the following —

Regarding conflict:

1) Conflict is fluid. It moves, changing like energy or the flow of a stream.

2) Conflict is created when one or more persons perceive from their viewpoint that it is operative. Often when I enter from the outside as a dispute resolution specialist, one of the parties will say, "There's nothing wrong here. There's nothing going on." I then speak to another party who says, "This is the worst conflict I've ever been in!"

We mediators know from experience that if one or more parties think that conflict exists, it does.

Years ago in a philosophy class, I learned about a sociologist named William Isaac Thomas (1863-1947) who developed the concept of *the definition of the situation.* In essence, one's irrational thinking becomes real to that person. Thomas taught that human beings *define* the situation in which they find themselves. For example, if people believe in trolls that live under bridges, they are real. If people believe that homosexuals are out to destroy the moral fiber of the United States, then for these people this perception is "fact." Thomas further noted that the world becomes fractioned into "me," "sort of like me" and "other." Once the label is applied, the "other" becomes a target of prejudice and discrimination.

Thus, we must always bear in mind that when one party perceives that conflict exists, to that person it does. Likewise, his or her individual viewpoint is as real as any fact ever presented. When you are in a conflict situation as a mediator, you must never minimize or denigrate your clients' perspectives, no matter how silly or prejudiced they may appear to be.

Regarding a dispute:
1) A dispute is more solid than the dynamic of conflict. It is something you can sink your teeth into. Unlike conflict which can be "managed," a dispute can be "settled."
2) Typically, a dispute is more or less tangible. It can be identified and named, and it is solvable — usually.

THE CRUM PERSPECTIVE
In the Western tradition, much has been written about the destructive nature of conflict. The Judeo-Christian tradition teaches us that conflict is rooted in sin. When Adam disobeyed God and ate the forbidden fruit, the first great conflict occurred. Traditional theology teaches that humankind "fell" into a state of sin and depravity. Then Cain killed his brother Abel. And so it goes. Many Christian denominations still preach that conflict is a visible manifestation of sin.

In *The Magic of Conflict,* Thomas Crum writes that conflict does not need to be destructive, but can provide an opportunity for growth and change, even a major breakthrough in one's otherwise mundane existence. Below, Crum gives us an excellent definition of conflict:

THE NATURE OF CONFLICT
Conflict is natural; neither positive nor negative. It just IS.

Conflict is just an interface pattern of energies.

Nature uses conflict as its primary motivator for change, creating beautiful beaches, canyons, mountains and pearls.

Conflict — Silent and Lurking

It's not whether you have conflict in your life. It's what you do with that conflict that makes a difference.

Conflict is not a contest.

Winning and losing are goals for games, not for conflicts.

Learning, growing and cooperating are goals for resolving conflicts.

Conflict can be seen as a gift of energy in which neither side loses and a new dance is created.

Resolving conflict is rarely about who is right. It *is* about acknowledgement and appreciation of differences.

Conflict begins within. As we unhitch the burden of belief systems and heighten our perceptions, we love more fully and freely.[3]

Conflict also can be a catalyst for social change. Imagine what would have happened had Rosa Parks gone to the back of the bus where she was "supposed to go." Rosa Parks said, "No!" A conflict ensued, and the whole world changed.

FIVE WAYS OF HANDLING CONFLICT

Now that we have a clearer understanding of what conflict is, how do individuals handle conflict? I have observed five methods people employ when encountering conflict in their everyday lives.

The first method is that of enforcement.

When I am in a conflict situation and I assume an enforcing mode, I want the rules followed. I expect the regulations to be carried out in every detail. I want to ensure that you do it my way.

The second mode for handling conflict is avoidance.

If I am in an avoiding mode, I seek to move away from the conflict. I need to get away from the fire as quickly as possible. Note that this is not the same as denial. In avoidance, I am aware of the conflict but make a conscious choice to avoid it.

The third mode for handling conflict is conciliation.

If I am in a conciliating mode, I will try to meet as many needs of the other party as possible. I will put my own needs aside or in second place in order to make peace.

The fourth mode for handling conflict is that of consensus building or collaboration.

In this mode, I want to identify as many needs and interests, including my own, that are operative in that conflict situation. Then I try to build a solution based on all of those needs. In consensus building, the best resolution will address as many of the needs of the persons present as possible.

The fifth way of handling conflict is that of bargaining or compromising.

When I am bargaining in a conflict situation, I start at point A, you start at point C, and we meet in the middle at point B. Compromising basically is incremental bargaining whereby we inch towards one another until a median is reached.

All of these are appropriate ways of handling conflict. Different situations call for different modes.

The *enforcing mode* is appropriate when the conflict has escalated to such a degree that it is out of hand. When the Ku Klux Klan and the Jewish marchers attempt to interface with each other, it is appropriate for security forces to move to keep peace and order, and to de-escalate the conflict. By enforcing a buffer zone, the safety of all is assured.

In a domestic violence episode when a woman is being beaten, this is not the time for consensus building. It is the time for avoidance. She needs to move away from that conflict situation as quickly as possible. Whenever safety issues are involved, *avoidance* is an appropriate way of dealing with conflict.

There are other conflict situations in which *conciliation* is important to use. It is Maurice and Josie's anniversary. Maurice strongly wants to go to a French restaurant. Josie has a taste for German cuisine. But Josie sees how important it is to Maurice that Josie go to the French restaurant. *The issue is not that important to Josie.* The relationship is more important than winning the argument. What does Josie do? She accommodates Maurice. Josie puts her need to have German food on hold because the other is so important to Maurice.

The most effective mode for handling conflict in a relationship is *collaboration.* These interconnections may be personal, professional, national or international. When relationships involve high stakes with long-term consequences, consensus building should be the preferred method.

Bargaining is appropriate when the stakes are low and the activity is fun. Usually a commodity is involved. A perfect example of bargaining in our culture is the ritual of buying a car. I visit the dealer, look at the sticker price, and see that it is inflated. Everybody in this culture knows the posted price is outrageous, including the salesperson. So I, as the buyer, enter the game of offering a ridiculously low figure for the car. We haggle back and forth until we agree on the price, generally somewhere in the middle.

Let us return to a more primitive mode of bargaining. It was a Friday night in the Old City of Jerusalem. A friend and I were shopping for Persian rugs. We went into shop after shop. At the time I knew nothing about Arab culture. Finally, I found three rugs I really wanted. The shopkeeper offered these rugs at an exorbitant price — $600. I told him I would pay $50. The game began. The negotiations continued for three hours over coffee. I finally bought the rugs for $200. When I returned to the States, the rugs were appraised at only $100. Such a deal! I was burned in this "bargain." (This was the same trip where my expert negotiation skills got me chased by another shop owner carrying a knife.)

Where else in America besides a car dealership can you engage in this back-and-forth? People do it all the time, often inappropriately, especially in relationships. Janis Joplin: "You can compromise yourself right out of existence."

For several years Congress has been locked in debate over the national debt. *Compromise* is the buzzword. The conflict handling mode that should be invoked is *collaboration*. Congress and the President must truly ascertain the interests and long-term needs of our country. Here are critical questions: What are the interests and the needs of the next generation? How will we as a country meet as many of these needs as is humanly possible? Have baby boomers performed corporate fiscal child abuse on the next generation? Giving up a few million here and pork barreling there will destroy this country.

We are drifting from the vision the founders of our country shaped in our Constitution and Bill of Rights when we "come to a compromise" that gives a piece of the pie to all the special interest groups. If we truly wish to address the national debt, health care problems and the condition of homeless people, then we must turn to a collaborative form of decision-making to resolve these social conflicts. Imagine a country which builds solutions based on the real needs of real people, rather than engaging in politics as usual — the politics of compromise.

FOUR

Three Tools for Diagnosing Conflict

Now that we have addressed this dynamic called conflict, it is important to understand that to deal with conflict, we need to diagnose the level of conflict, whether the conflict is healthy or unhealthy, and the type of conflict. Here are three tools to accomplish this objective.

1) CONFLICT INTENSITY SCALE

On October 17, 1989, I was driving into the San Francisco Bay area. It was a magnificent fall day. The sky was perfectly blue, the air was still, and the temperature was comfortable. As I approached the Bay Bridge from the Oakland side, the earth began to shake, the bridge started to tremble, the birds stopped singing, and traffic came to a dead halt. My car radio went off the air. The 7.1 earthquake had hit. I spent the next three days in the midst of a natural and human disaster: huge fires; no electricity, which created a haunting darkness; fear; acts of kindness and scenes of ugliness.

Later, I reflected on the immense power of that earthquake. It was a conflict of massive forces meeting and fighting for space, of giant earth plates scraping against each other — a raw elemental conflict of great magnitude.

The Richter Scale is applied to measure the intensity of an earthquake. A Level 2 earthquake is not very serious. It measures the natural changing and shifting of the earth's surface. At a Level 7 earthquake, the seriousness is readily apparent. In Southern California, newspapers run a seismo-watch. In one normal and representative week in 1993, 74 seismic events hit that region.

As with earthquakes, conflicts have certain degrees of intensity. Each conflict has its own inherent level. To measure these levels, I have developed an intensity scale to apply to each conflict situation. Use it as a diagnostic tool.

The Conflict Intensity Scale

Code 1.0–1.9: This is a Low-Grade Conflict, like a low-grade fever. In a Code 1 conflict, the situation is characterized by dis-ease and a sense of discomfort.

An example of a 1.0 is a marriage in which the parties have been together for 40 years. The last time they spoke to each other was when the children left for college 20 years ago. (I have worked with people who haven't talked for that length of time.) If you ask these folks, they will say, "There's nothing wrong here." But something does not feel right to you, the mediator. It is probably a Code 1 conflict.

Another example of a Code 1: You are brought in by the president of a corporation as a troubleshooter to work with a department that has problems. You visit that department and people say, "There's no problem here." But the atmosphere does not feel right to you, although there is no clearly identifiable problem. As a mediator, you will want to probe the true feelings of the parties involved and try to "get it all out." This may escalate the conflict to the point where it can be identified and dealt with.

Code 2.0–2.9: This is a Problem-To-Be-Solved. This degree is characterized by the parties acknowledging that an issue exists that needs resolution. In a Code 2 the disputants focus on resolving the problem, not attacking one another, as in higher intensity conflicts. Those involved have a genuine desire to solve the problem, to effectuate wholeness, to bring closure, and then move on. Collaboration is an appropriate mode for handling a Code 2.

Several younger members of the First Church of Oldetown want to move from their decaying downtown location to the southwest quadrant of the city where new families are moving in, and the population is booming. They want to build a new church. The older members want to stay to preserve the history, the rootedness, of the 100-year-old building. The two sides clash. In a Code 2 conflict, the people of First Church will come together and acknowledge that the issue of whether or not to relocate needs to be addressed, refraining from launching personal attacks in the process. They will explore options to solve the problem, and frame a solution.

Code 3.0–3.9: This is a Debate. In a debate the goal is to persuade the other side. If I am in a debate with you, my purpose is to lay out my facts and to convince you that I am right and you are wrong. Your goal is the same. We are both clear about this mode of action. In a debate, one begins to see the blurring of personalities with the problems. The debate attitude: "Because you do not grasp the superiority of my method, your intelligence level, by definition, leaves much room for improvement."

Emotions start to cloud the issues and muddy the waters. In a Code 3 conflict, intermittent anger may be present, and you may begin to see inappropriate humor. Racist and sexist remarks often creep in.

A classic example of a Code 3 conflict is the debate format within our legislative process. Debate is the legislative form of solving problems. Litigation in the courts is another example.

Code 4.0–4.9: This is a serious Win/Lose Competition. The fight is on! This conflict is characterized by a move to win at the expense of the other side. By definition, in a Code 4, I am going to win and you will, of course, lose. Both parties strive to win, win, win! Lines are clearly drawn. Factions are formed, with the folk in the white hats against the folk in the black hats. You are either with me or you are against me. The employee parking lot and the workplace coffee room are the sites of clandestine caucuses. The combatants often refuse to confront each other eyeball to eyeball. Instead, they line up the troops. Positions form and solidify.

I was called in to resolve a dispute in a medical office. The receptionist and the office manager despised each other. The receptionist approached one group of doctors, describing the laziness and incompetence of the office manager. The office manager triangulated with another group of doctors, delineating the abrasiveness and controlling qualities of the receptionist. When I came in, they were at a 4.5 level. The two principals were not speaking to each other. They had their soldiers in formation. The receptionist and the office manager had wreaked havoc in that office, garnering support at luncheon meetings to the point where the medical practice had split into two parts.

Code 5.0–5.9: This is the Fight/Flight code. This conflict is marked by hostility in the form of verbal and sometimes physical abuse, as we move up the scale to the 5.7-5.9 level. Problems are no longer the focus. Persons become the issue. Individuals are named and attacked. In the upper level of a 5.0, dissolution of the relationship is the norm. The "other" becomes the enemy, and the goal is to harm. I will either stay and fight you, and typically hurt you, or I will extricate myself from the situation and avoid you at all costs. You have become a non-entity in my life. I bury you.

I worked once with a highly religious family in conflict. One of the young adult children had performed a sufficiently heinous act. The family held a funeral ritual and announced, "Our son is dead." The child was symbolically destroyed. His name was never to be mentioned. He no longer existed.

The best example of a Code 5 in our culture is adversarial divorce. The film *The War of the Roses* is an archetypal example of divorce, American style, in which the parties destroy each other, their property, their goods, their relationship, their real estate, all in the name of "getting even." They attack, and then flee to their attorneys to plan their next attack. They spend their fortunes in order to demolish their life partner.

A newspaper account of Code 5 activity provided by the Southern Poverty Law Center shows the extent of damages on this scale:

- In 1989, two women, one black and one white, moved out of the Jacksonville, Florida, mobile home they shared for two months after facing hate mail, racial slurs, vandalism and burglary of their home, and a cross burning. The neighborhood they were living in was solidly white.

Code 6.0–6.9: The operative for this code is Search and Destroy. This level is characterized by a total breakdown in communication. Parties will not speak to one another. Misinformation or disinformation is rampant. A depersonalization of the other party emerges. In a Code

6.0, disputants begin to identify the "other" as *evil*. By the time conflict escalates to this level, emotions may be steely cold.

Listen to the rhetoric of the neo-Nazis. Their emotions often are cold and self-righteous and crisp, as clean as a flame. They may speak of blacks or Jews or homosexuals. But they use a matter-of-fact tone as they preach, "We must wipe the earth clean of this filth."

I mediated a dispute between the Ku Klux Klan and a Jewish group. The Jews were very emotional over the issue, extremely expressive verbally and physically, using strong gesticulations. The Klan group sat motionless at the table. They were colder than steel. In a Code 6, there is a sense of self-righteousness and arrogance. *To show emotion is to engage. The enemy is not worthy of being engaged at a personal level. The job is to search out the enemy and to destroy it.*

Two more newspaper accounts give you the feel of a Code 6 level of conflict:

- In 1990, four churches with predominantly black congregations were arsoned in Louisville, Kentucky.
- In 1989, BB gun pellets were fired at the house of a Chinese-American in Arcadia, California, causing $1,800 in damages. A cross was burned outside the home.[4]

Code 7.0–7.9: This level is Annihilation. It is characterized by literally wiping out other people, the total destruction of the "other." In a Code 7.0 conflict, complete destruction is the goal. Suicide, the Holocaust and war are examples of this intensity of conflict. Suicide is the ultimate self-annihilation; and nuclear war is the ultimate social conflict.

Recently, I was privileged to visit the Holocaust Museum in Washington, D.C. There I was confronted with images of 7.9 conflict: videos of medical torture; a mountain of shoes ripped from victims before they were gassed; photos of naked, emaciated piles of human flesh; and camp artifacts with the stench of rotting skin.

Currently in our world the ethnic cleansing that is taking place in Bosnia-Herzegovina is an example of a Code 7. Gang warfare in our streets is another.

Two newspaper accounts of Code 7 carnage:

- In 1990, a New Orleans white youth, his body covered with satanic and white supremacy tattoos, was charged with murdering a 59-year-old black woman because she pulled away from a stop sign too slowly.
- In 1990, a white man was indicted for 70 criminal offenses in connection with two bombings. In the first, a federal judge was killed by a bomb mailed to his home in Birmingham, Alabama. Two days later, a black attorney in Savannah, Georgia, was killed by a similar mail bomb.[5]

For myself, the most appropriate cases for mediation fall into the range of a Code 1.0 through a Code 5.9. A mediator must be able to assess the intensity of any conflict and to step down if the conflict has escalated beyond control and the case is too intense for mediation...or if it is beyond the skill level of the mediator.

When you the mediator diagnose a conflict, different parties may be locked in (and often are) at different levels. If this is the case, you must intervene at the *highest* level, address the conflict *first* at this level, then try to de-escalate the conflict to a mediable level.

The Richter Scale is a logarithmic scale. When an earthquake moves from a Code 1 to a Code 2, the intensity is 100 times greater. The same exponential factor of 100 is present when a conflict intensifies from a Code 2 to a Code 3. A Code 7.0 is logarithmically thousands of times more intense than a Code 2. Remember this fact.

2) THE HEALTHY VS. UNHEALTHY CONFLICT INDEX

This diagnostic tool involves the process of discerning the difference between healthy and unhealthy conflict. As mentioned earlier, much emphasis has been placed on unhealthy conflict in our society. When I enter into a conflicted situation, I want to discover how the people involved deal with conflict.

First, if the disputing parties see conflict as wrong or sinful, they will deal with conflict in an unhealthy way. If the disputants view conflict as inevitable, or as a chance to grow, then they have a healthy view toward conflict.

Second, in an unhealthy conflict situation, the disputants quickly mix people and problems together. They cannot separate the people from the problems. In a healthy conflict situation, the disputants are clearly able to see the difference. They focus on issues.

They may say, "Susan, our relationship is important to me, still I do not agree with you on this issue." Or, "You and I see this issue of homosexual rights from different perspectives."

Third, in a healthy conflicted situation, open communication is the norm. The more healthy you and I are when in conflict, the more we look one another in the eye, the more we speak directly to one another, and the more we listen.

In an unhealthy conflicted situation, communication is diminished. When disputants interrelate in an unhealthy way, people talk about each other behind backs, do not confront each other directly, and try to form coalitions with like-minded people.

Fourth, how long is the balance sheet? In healthy conflict situations, the ledger is short. The principals address the issue at hand, not what transpired in their relationship 20 years ago. In unhealthy conflicted systems, the grievance list is long. It grows by the day. Not only do I remember what you did to me and how you wronged me five years ago, but I vividly recall what you said to my friends 18 years ago.

Fifth, unhealthy conflict has reactive interaction. I write a memo to you and you immediately fire back a nasty letter to me.

In a healthy conflicted system, the atmosphere is interactive. There is a give and take, an exchange of ideas, and a spirit of cooperation and openness. When Person A writes a memo, Person B will think before responding to the issues contained in the memo. In an interactive atmosphere, you will see a great deal of careful listening and thought-out statements.

The sixth element I look for to diagnose a conflicted situation is that, in an unhealthy conflicted system, the disputants tend to ignore the problems and deny what is going on. In a healthy system, the parties acknowledge the existence of a problem and the need to solve it.

Seventh, in an unhealthy system, there is a strong need to solve the problem too quickly. The disputants are very solution-oriented. They do not want to feel the pain of the conflict and say, "Let's get it over with, bring closure to it." In a healthy conflicted system, there is a sense of *kairos,* the Greek word for God's time. *Chronos* is clock time where persons allocate a certain amount of time to solve a problem. They are bound by the hands on the clock. *Kairos* does not have a clock. Resolution takes as much time as is needed. The parties involved take the time to go through the journey together, to experience the pain, to acknowledge it, and to come out together on the other side.

I am indebted to the work of the Mennonites and Tom Crum in helping me see the difference between constructive and destructive, or toxic, conflict within systems. The Mennonite Conciliation Service offers a wonderful video entitled *Conflict in the Church,* which demonstrates many of the above principles. I recommend it.

3) A TAXONOMY OF CONFLICT

The third diagnostic tool I use for assessing every conflict situation is a taxonomy of conflict. Taxonomy is a system for classifying. There are six types of conflicts.

Substantive conflicts are conflicts which involve commodities, resources and "things." A rancher claimed that he owned the rights to the water under his ranch. A large corporation also laid claim to these water rights. This formed the boundaries of the dispute. Salary disputes are also examples of substantive conflict.

Psychological conflicts are brought on by intra-psychic disruptions. An individual may have an emotional problem that creates conflict, often internally and externally. The conflict is self-generated. Examples are alcohol, drug and sexual addictions. I spoke to a man who was a sex addict. He described what he went through. He felt compelled every day to find a sexual liaison. I asked what were his needs. "To feel like I'm valid. To feel loved," he said. However, when he engaged in sex, he would feel extreme guilt and shame. He was never happy. Also, those around a person with psychological conflicts will feel the pain acted out on them by the individual.

Relationship conflicts are found in inter-personal relationships. Jonathan and Linda are having marital difficulties. They fight over religion, money and the children. In this example, there are *three* parties: Jonathan, Linda and their relationship. The relationship is hurting and breaking. If reconciliation is to occur, then the *relationship* must be treated not just the people.

Information conflicts are created when different parties within a system have access to different data. No one has the same set of facts. Church organizations are beset with these problems. Information is not readily put on the table. Gossip is rampant, misinformation explodes throughout the system, and conflict is the result.

In a midwestern Protestant church association which covers two states, four prominent members of the regional governing body stole $40 million from the church credit union. When the scandal broke, the leadership did not communicate the facts to their constituents, but remained silent. The confused people invented their own scenarios of the theft. The result was chaos. This conflict created extreme pain, brokenness, anger, shame and guilt. Many withdrew, thinking that the entire church was tainted instead of the four guilty parties.

Information conflicts happen in all sorts of organizations not just religious bodies.

System conflicts are created by poor structures, whether the structure be a family, organization or corporation. A structure can create barriers between people, power imbalances or destructive behavioral interactions. Ill-defined job descriptions in a business often spawn these conflicts. Party A does not know what she is supposed to be doing. Neither does Party B. Both are floundering on the job, getting in each other's way and becoming very angry at each other. It is the fault of the system for not providing clearly-defined and delineated job descriptions. Or the lines of accountability are fuzzy.

In a family situation, a mother may not tell her children how she wants the chores to be done. She yells at the children for not performing their duties. The children are frustrated because they are anxious to please their mother and are met with anger. Their job descriptions were not clearly defined!

Value conflicts occur at a fundamental level in the way people view the essence of life. The conflict comes out of different philosophies, world views and ethics. An example is a marriage in which the wife is Jewish and the husband is a member of a New Age group. When they enter the marriage, they have a "live and let live" attitude. The children are born. Then religious perspectives soon rear their heads: "How are we going to raise these children?"

Another example is abortion. During a pro-life protest outside an abortion clinic in Pensacola, Florida, a local man prayed for the doctor to "give his life to Jesus," then shot him three times in the back as the doctor stepped out of his car. The 47-year-old practitioner died in the hospital during surgery. The anti-abortion activist calmly surrendered to the authorities and was charged with murder.

In every conflict situation, it is important for the mediator to apply this taxonomy. Often a conflict will combine several of these six types of conflict. A primarily substantive conflict, for example, may also involve relationship and information conflicts. As a professional mediator, you must be able to untangle these classifications.

We have just completed an overview of the three diagnostic tools I use in assessing each dispute I mediate: the Conflict Intensity Scale, the Healthy Vs. Unhealthy Conflict Index, and the Taxonomy of Conflict.

IN ESSENCE...

- Mediation, not violence, is the sane way to resolve disputes.

- Conflict is to be found in all walks of life.

- Our culture denies and fears conflict because of its scary, unknown qualities.

- Conflict, once defined, loses its terror.

- People handle conflict in five ways: enforcement, avoidance, conciliation, collaboration and bargaining.

- The three tools for diagnosing conflict are:
  1) the Conflict Intensity Scale
  2) the Healthy vs. Unhealthy Conflict Index
  3) the Taxonomy of Conflict.

NOTES

1. *From Conflict to Resolution,* by Susan Heitler, Ph.D. (W. W. Norton & Company, 1990).

2. *From Conflict to Resolution,* by Susan Heitler, Ph.D. (W. W. Norton & Company, 1990, p.5).

3. *The Magic of Conflict,* by Thomas F. Crum (Touchstone Books, Simon & Schuster, 1987, p.49).

4. Founded in 1971, the Southern Poverty Law Center is a nonprofit foundation supported by private donations. The Center's Klanwatch project was formed in 1980 to help curb Klan and racist violence through litigation, education and monitoring. To this date, at least seven major lawsuits have resulted in indictments and civil suit judgments against hate groups in the United States.

5. See note 4.

PART TWO

The Great Earthshake or
Surviving the Epicenter
of a Paradigm Shift

The Paradigm Shift

FIVE

From Traditional Paradigm to New Paradigm

Gore Vidal said, "For certain people after 50, litigation takes the place of sex." We in the Western culture have been imprisoned in the grip of a litigation paradigm that is now out of hand. The United States is the most litigious nation in the world. We have more attorneys per capita than any other country on earth.

In 1992, *Business Week* featured a cover story on the glut of lawyers and came up with some interesting statistics. For every 100,000 people in the U.S., we have 307.4 lawyers. That's one lawyer for every 325 people. Britain has 102.7 per 100,000, Germany has 82 and Japan has 12.1 per 100,000. In Japan, that's one attorney for 8264 people.

Our situation is worsening. In 1971 we had 355,242 lawyers practicing, in 1980 the ranks swelled to 542,205, in 1990 the number reached 750,000, and in the year 2000 we will have one million lawyers unless we change our dispute resolution habits. Lawsuits in America rose from 14.1 million in 1984 to 15.5 million in 1986 to 16.6 million in 1988 to 18.4 million in 1990.

Business is taking a stand against these rising civil suits. A full 83 percent of corporate executives say their decisions are more and more affected by the threat of lawsuits, and 62 percent say the legal system hampers America's ability to compete in the world market. These executives put the blame on generous juries, plaintiffs and the contingency-fee system. Most (97 percent) lean to such alternative methods as arbitration, mediation and private judges to resolve disputes.

What does Japan do? To quote directly from *Business Week:*

JAPAN'S APPROACH

- Limits the number of attorneys passing the bar exam to two percent of 35,000 applicants.
- Forces would-be plaintiffs to pay an up-front fee to their lawyers of up to eight percent of damages sought.
- Bars contingency fees, class actions and other fee-sharing devices that make it easier to sue.
- Lets judges, not juries, set damage awards, which rarely exceed $150,000, even when the victim has been killed.
- Bans discovery so that plaintiffs are denied access before trial to an opponent's potential evidence.
- Nurtures a strong cultural attitude that confrontation is to be avoided and looks down upon those who sue.[1]

The butt of humor often represents displeasure. Attorney jokes have been around since Shakespeare and continue to flood the psyche of the American people. Here is one. (I can't resist.)

A plane crashed carrying a priest, a doctor and a lawyer. Upon arriving at the Heavenly Gate, Saint Peter announced that since the crash was unexpected, they would have to consult Jesus about their eternal rewards.

The priest approached Jesus. "What do you want as your reward?" asked Jesus.

"Oh, my Lord, only to sit at your right hand," the priest replied.

"Granted," said Jesus.

Next the doctor approached the throne. "What do you want as your reward?" asked Jesus.

"Oh Father, only to sit at your left hand," said the doctor.

"Granted," said Jesus.

The lawyer was the last one to approach the throne. "What do you want as your reward?" Jesus asked.

There was a brief pause. Then the lawyer, looking at the chair, said: "Get up!"[2]

Change is releasing the vice-like grip of the adversarial system. We are in the midst of a quiet revolution, a vast paradigm shift. In *Future Edge: Discovering the New Paradigms of Success,* page 32, Joel Barker defines a paradigm:

A paradigm is a set of rules and regulations (written or unwritten) that does two things: (1) it establishes or defines boundaries; and (2) it tells you how to behave inside the boundaries in order to be successful.

Barker then posits a paradigm shift as a change to a different set of rules, as working within new parameters. On page 39, Barker states, "...when the rules change, the whole world can change." Only pioneers have the guts to stand alone: "Those who choose to change their paradigms early do it not as an act of the head but as an act of the heart."[3]

We are gradually emerging from the old litigation paradigm to a new archetype within the parameters of dispute resolution — the paradigm of alternative dispute resolution. It is new in that the American people have not been exposed to its benefits until recently. Yet it is enduring in the sense that various forms of mediation and arbitration have been used throughout the ages in many cultures to settle disputes.

This paradigm has recently been labeled "Alternative Dispute Resolution (ADR)." I strongly dislike this tag in that it connotes an alternative to litigation. It is as if mediation and arbitration are ancillary court functions or quasi-legal endeavors. They are NOT. Perhaps a better term would be "Effective Dispute Resolution" or, simply, "Dispute Resolution." But, alas, Alternative Dispute Resolution has stuck. And so, I use the term ADR...reluctantly.

The new ADR paradigm is superior to the traditional litigation paradigm in several ways. First, it is less expensive. For example, litigation generally costs three times more than a mediated settlement.

The emotional savings are mammoth, as well.

Second, the ADR paradigm is expeditious. Often, 12 to 18 months go by before a claimant can get his or her case heard in court. Normally, one can enter an alternative dispute settlement method within 30 days of filing.

Third, the ADR paradigm declares that disputes belong first to the people, not the courts. Responsibility falls back onto individual parties to work out their own problems.

Fourth, the ADR paradigm asserts that people need to be empowered to come to resolutions on their own whenever possible. For too long, citizens have abdicated their personal power to the courts to settle differences. Generally, people know what is best for their own lives, and desire to retain personal power.

Fifth, unlike litigation which provides cookie cutter solutions which treat people like interchangeable parts in a clogged machine, the ADR paradigm demands that every dispute be resolved in a manner that is customized and crafted to the unique needs of the affected parties.

This shift in paradigms has been demonstrated by several recent surveys. One study conducted in the early 1990s by the National Institute for Dispute Resolution (NIDR), noted that 42 percent of the public with minimal education on the subject would likely use ADR, and an additional 40 percent were "somewhat likely." Later, after receiving a short explanation of litigation, mediation and arbitration, 62 percent of those polled stated they would use a mediator rather than go to court, and 54 percent would see an arbitrator.

The same NIDR poll noted that 45 percent of those polled were first inclined to "leave a confrontation alone," and 41 percent preferred to discuss the issue directly. To arrive at a fair conclusion was important to 41 percent, and 21 percent placed importance on active participation in the resolution. *At the end of the interviews, 80 percent chose ADR over litigation.*

"Our work is cut out," said NIDR spokesperson Martha Barnett. "To achieve the broader potential, the public must learn about dispute resolution."

The American Arbitration Association publishes a pamphlet, "A Guide to Mediation for Business People." Following are some of the benefits of mediation listed:

- Parties are directly engaged in negotiating the settlement.
- The mediator, as a neutral third party, can view the dispute objectively and can assist the parties in exploring alternatives that they might not have considered on their own.
- Parties enhance the possibility of continuing a business relationship with each other.
- Creative solutions or accommodations to special needs of the parties may become part of the settlement.

In another study, the Northern California Mediation Center explored the reasons of 106 couples who chose to mediate their divorces:

- To reach an overall agreement satisfactory to both me and my spouse (91 percent).
- To reduce or avoid hostility between me and my spouse (83 percent).
- To reduce the cost of obtaining the divorce (82 percent).
- To reduce contact with lawyers and court proceedings (81 percent).
- To want a fair property division agreement (70 percent).
- To retain a friendly relationship with my spouse (65 percent).

In still another poll by the California Judicial Council, in a short article entitled, "Lawyers Like Court System Better Than Public Does," the poll stated that "52 percent of Californians had an 'only fair' or 'poor' opinion of the state's court system — but only 21 percent of the attorneys surveyed thought so poorly of the system."[4]

There is a new vision in the land. Listen to what Chief Justice Warren E. Burger said in, "Isn't There A Better Way?" (*Annual Report on the State of the Judiciary,* January 24, 1982):

The obligation of our profession is, or long has thought to be, to serve as healers of human conflicts. To fulfill our traditional obligation means that we should provide mechanisms that can produce an acceptable result in the shortest possible time, with the least possible expense and with a minimum of stress on the participants. That is what justice is all about....

Law schools have traditionally steeped the students in the adversary tradition rather than the skills of resolving conflicts....

One reason our courts have become overburdened is that Americans are increasingly turning to the courts for relief from a range of personal distresses and anxieties. Remedies for personal wrongs that once were considered the responsibility of institutions other than the courts are now boldly asserted as legal "entitlements." The courts have been expected to fill the void created by the decline of church, family and neighborhood unity....

We read in the news of cases that continue not weeks or months, but years....We must now use the inventiveness, the ingenuity and the resourcefulness that have long characterized the American business and legal community to shape new tools. The paradox is that we already have some very good tools and techniques ready and waiting for imaginative lawyers to adapt them to current needs.[5]

Many people dream of what a dispute resolution system for the 21st century will look like. In the Winter 1992 issue of *NIDR Forum*, David L. Tevelin reported on a conference attended by more than 300 judges, attorneys, social scientists, doctors, futurists, court administrators and other professionals. A main topic was the future of ADR.

Some looked to traditional litigation with emphasis on due process and individual rights. Others saw ADR in a prominent role but under court supervision. A third group projected a "multi-door" judicial system with many options that did not require legal representation. Patrons would take out "judicare" insurance, and ADR would be accessible 24 hours a day, at malls and via home delivery.[6]

In his article, Tevelin quoted the futuristic views of Jim Dator and Sharon Rodgers, from the perspective of an observer living in the year 2020:

The facilities of justice centers are now almost as ubiquitous in time and place as the old gasoline stations of the

1960s, or the fast-food restaurants of the 1980s. And so is their style of service. Nowadays, the needs and desires of the customer always come first, and service is prompt, efficient and friendly....

Some of these neighborhood justice centers feature banks of artificially-intelligent (AI) expert systems for conflict resolution advice and assistance. Voice responsive interactive computers with one-quarter life-sized holographic display capabilities literally walk customers through a variety of resolution situations before assisting the customers in choosing a technique, or set of techniques, which enable them to solve their disputes — wholly without "live" human involvement, except for the persons in dispute themselves.[7]

In conclusion, Tevelin noted that many of the prominent judges and lawyers educated in the adversarial justice system underwent a paradigm shift during the five-day conference. Education, thus, is the key. "The new ADR paradigm, however, will need to be a part of not only legal education, but public education as well, from grade school on up," he stated.

Langston Hughes, a truly great American poet, wrote in *Dream Boogie* (1951):

> What happens to a dream deferred?
> Does it dry up
> like a raisin in the sun?
> Or fester like a sore —
> And then run?
> Does it stink like rotten meat?
> Or crust and sugar over —
> like a syrupy sweet?
>
> Maybe it just sags
> like a heavy load.
>
> Or does it explode?

The dream of a new way for settling disputes will not be deferred any longer. It is exploding here and now. In the words of Victor Hugo:

"There is one thing stronger than all the armies in the world: and that is an idea whose time has come."

And remember what Joel Barker wrote: "...when the rules change, the whole world can change."[8]

The old rules came into play during the sad Woody Allen/Mia Farrow courtroom spectacle that cheapened two great film artists. The fight was over custody of their three children. In the courtroom we sadly learned that: "Farrow is a shrill, psychotic, frigid witch" (Allen's version); and, "Allen is a perverted, child-groping absentee dad" (Farrow's version).

According to *Rocky Mountain News* columnist Alan Dershowitz, the rocky road had started out bumpless. Dershowitz was successfully mediating a meeting between the lawyers of the two parties, covering visitation rights and financial issues. "It was a very conventional settlement discussion, typical in matrimonial cases," Dershowitz wrote in his column.

During the meeting, however, Woody Allen filed a lawsuit seeking sole custody of the children and then held a press conference, announcing to the world that he was accused of molesting his adopted daughter. In Dershowitz's words:

> The end result of Woody's lawsuit is now known throughout the world. It was an unequivocal defeat for him and potential disaster for his career. He ended up far worse than he would have in any reasonable settlement. The judge declared him to be a person with "no parenting skills," who knew almost nothing about his children's lives...and who is "self-absorbed, untrustworthy and insensitive...."

> Woody Allen must now be kicking himself for not continuing the settlement discussions he cut off. Indeed, following his defeat, he offered to sit down and talk. But it is too late to undo the damage to him, to the children and to Farrow that resulted from going public in the first place.

> I suspect that Woody Allen's next movie may be about the virtues of alternative dispute resolution — settling cases without the need for public litigation.[9]

Perhaps Gore Vidal was correct in his own time and place, in reference to sex and litigation beyond the age of 50. But given the shift to a faster, more stress-free paradigm of dispute resolution, we in this burgeoning new field affirm that, for certain people after the age of twenty-five, alternative dispute resolution will take the place of lawsuits...but never sex.

SIX

Basic Principles upon Which the ADR Paradigm is Based

The "new" alternative dispute resolution paradigm is based upon several basic principles. In *From Conflict to Resolution*, Susan Heitler cites three characteristics of effectively resolved conflicts:

- The process is based on talking, not verbal or physical violence.
- The process is predominantly cooperative, not avoidant, competitive, antagonistic or coercive.
- The outcome is a settlement that all participants find acceptable and that addresses the concerns of all participants.[10]

In *Getting to Yes*, Fisher and Ury offer this insight:

Any method of negotiation may be fairly judged by three criteria: It should produce a wise agreement if agreement is possible. It should be efficient. And it should improve or at least not damage the relationship between the parties. (A wise agreement can be defined as one which meets the legitimate interests of each side to the extent possible, resolves conflicting interests fairly, is durable, and takes community interests into account.)[11]

The litigation paradigm says that there must be a winner and a loser. The new paradigm teaches that a win-win solution often exists, which means that as many of the interests and needs of the parties are met as possible. This cross-stitching effect, connecting the underlying interests of the disputants, creates a foundation for all parties to win.

Heitler describes resolution as follows:

Resolution refers to the attainment of a solution that satisfies the requirements of all of the seemingly conflicting forces and thereby produces a feeling of closure for all participants....

Psychological resolution exists when two or more apparently contradictory elements have been transformed into one element that exists without opposition. As in mathematical resolution, what looked complex has been transformed to apparent simplicity. As in music, the feeling tones switch from dissonance to consonance. As in literature, at the point of resolution oppositions give way to solution and a feeling that all has been settled. The drama seems over. All has been decided.[12]

The traditional paradigm is predicated on position-based bargaining. Each party begins with an opening position. Then the parties "edge toward" one another until a compromise is reached.

Position-based bargaining may be useful and appropriate in exchanging commodities. But it is inappropriate and often destructive in conflicts involving business connections, personal relationships, disputes involving community issues, and fights where third parties are involved (children, for example).

What is a position? A position is the solution to a problem to which one party has come after analyzing all the data available to that party using the best of his or her ability according to their particular history, background and personal criteria. The new paradigm requires that one go beneath the positions to discover what the underlying needs and interests are. How did a person get to that position? I call this function *interest-based problem solving*.

I conclude this chapter with a vision of a world that moves to the rhythm of the new paradigm, taken from the book *Dispute Resolution: Negotiation, Mediation, and Other Processes.* ADR would strive:

- To lower court caseloads and expenses.
- To reduce the parties' expenses and time.
- To provide speedy settlement of those disputes that were disruptive of the community or the lives of the parties' families.
- To improve the public's satisfaction with the justice system.
- To encourage resolutions that were suited to the parties' needs.
- To increase voluntary compliance with resolutions.
- To restore the influence of neighborhood and community values and the cohesiveness of communities.
- To provide accessible forums to people with disputes.
- To teach the public to try more effective processes than violence or litigation for settling disputes.[13]

SEVEN

The Language of Dispute Resolution

It is important for professionals in the field to have an understanding of the language of alternative dispute resolution. Many of these words traditionally have been employed in the context of social conversation, thus creating confusion in the minds of the public. People tend to confuse "mediation" with "arbitration," and "arbitration" with "fact finding." The media constantly interchange "mediation" and "arbitration." These words need to attain refined meaning in their new context.

A GLOSSARY OF TERMS

Arbitration: A dispute resolution methodology in which a neutral intermediary convenes the disputing parties, hears testimony, receives evidence, and renders a binding decision.

Arbitrator: The neutral intermediary who conducts the arbitration hearing and is the decision-maker in the dispute.

Conciliation: The process of bringing disputing parties to the point where they agree to work out their dispute, generally through self-negotiation. This process may involve some other dispute resolution method if required.

Facilitate: To make easy or easier; to assist; to help.

Fact Finding: A process whereby an intermediary investigates the issues in dispute and submits a report of findings and recommendations for action. The process is informal and the recommendations are non-binding.

Interests: Perceived needs, fears, concerns and wants; that which goes into creating a "position" for the parties within a dispute.

Intermediary: A person who is not a direct party to a dispute who intervenes to settle the dispute.

Litigation: The process of settling a dispute in a secular court or administrative unit according to rules, regulations and law.

Mediation: A dispute resolution methodology in which a neutral intermediary assists disputing parties to come to an agreement with which they can live.

Mediator: The neutral intermediary who conducts the mediation process and facilitates the parties to come to their own solutions and settlement. The mediator has no decision-making authority.

Negotiation: The process whereby disputants work out an agreement between or among themselves.

Neutral: Impartial; is not a stakeholder in the dispute; has no connection to the issues in conflict. Must be perceived as neutral and actually be neutral.

Position: A stance, demand, posture. A SOLUTION to which a party has come on his or her own after processing all data available to said party.

This book focuses on mediation as a way of resolving disputes in more effective and healthier avenues. Remember, mediation is a non-adversarial process in which a neutral third party meets with persons in conflict, the primary goal being to help them settle their dispute. The solution, as well as the dispute, belongs to the parties. The mediator does not have the power to impose a settlement. The only real authority a mediator has is that given the mediator by the parties to guide the settlement process.

MEDIATION FORUMS AND TYPES

I am often asked what types of disputes can best be settled through mediation. Mediation works well in such family disputes as divorce, child custody and post-divorce modifications. Mediation is effective in conflict over eldercare: adult siblings may be severely conflicted over whether to put an elderly member of the family in a nursing home. Parent-teen conflicts are ripe for mediation. Virtually any type of domestic issue can be handled in mediation.

Workplace disputes such as employer-employee concerns and issues of sexual harassment and other forms of prohibited discrimination are appropriate for mediation. Salary disputes and early retirement offers are prime candidates.

Disputes which cover questions of product liability, personal injury cases, neighbor-neighbor disputes and relationship disputes are excellent for mediation. For example, a gay couple living together elects to dissolve the relationship and separate their property. Their case would not be recognized as a marriage and not considered a divorce in a court of law. But mediation can be very helpful in this situation.

Mediation is also effective in church and synagogue disputes where people are connected to each other in a community of faith. The list goes on. The bottom line is that wherever two or more people are gathered and are in dispute with one another, the dispute may lend itself very well to the mediation process.

Now let us examine situations where you may want to refer a case to a colleague. You may not be neutral about the issues being mediated. Once I supervised a mediator who was called in to resolve an environmental problem involving multiple parties. The mediator was a staunch environmentalist and against development. When she realized that she was biased, she excused herself from the case. Biases may include civil rights issues, gender issues, sexual orientation, political leanings and others. Be aware of your biases. Know yourself.

You or one of the disputing parties may find yourselves in physical danger. Domestic violence cases or highly volatile intensity levels during any case are red flags. If safety issues arise, you may wish to step down from the case. Common sense and discernment are needed.

EIGHT

A Brief History of Time (ADR Time, That is)

Many of us in the profession act as if alternative dispute resolution was invented 10 years ago. Not so. It probably began one evening by the campfire, with two cavemen grunting over the day's hunting expedition:

Rof: That deer you knocked out was MINE.

Lof: No. (snort, grunt.) MINE!

Rof: Was not.

Lof: Was too.

Rof: Was not.

The wise woman of the tribe arose and walked over to the fire, gazed serenely at her kin and said, "Rof! Lof! You are brothers! You BOTH must hunt for us to survive. Now you two settle this and let's all have something to eat."

This is my fantasy of how ADR began historically. Now, to recorded history...

The word *mediation* is derived from the Latin words *medi* or *medio*, which mean "middle." In ancient Rome, a job description called for a *mediastinus,* which meant "a helper standing in the middle of." In classical Christian theology, Jesus Christ is seen as the mediator between God and humankind. In 1667 John Milton wrote: "All mankind must have been lost had not the Son of God his dearest mediation thus renewed." Christ was the ultimate mediator in classical theology — bringing together God and humanity.[14]

Early on, mediation was a scientific and mathematical term. In 1425, its definition was: "Mediacion is a takyng out of halfe a nombre out of a holle nombre." In 1542 from the Greek: "Mediation...is nothyng els but deuidying [dividing] by two." In chemistry, a substance interjected into the chemical process is called a mediator.[15]

A friend told me that mediation was used in ancient Egypt. It is recorded that two neighbors were in dispute. The king asked a third neighbor to meet with the two to resolve it.

In the Christian tradition, Chapter 18 of Matthew clearly delineates a step-by-step process by which Christians are called upon to resolve their disputes outside the court system. It states that people in conflict are to come together on a one-on-one basis to strive to work out their problem. If that fails, they are to bring witnesses to the dispute in order to resolve their differences. If that also does not succeed, they are to bring their dispute to the church body so that a resolution can be reached.

In mythology, the three squabbling goddesses asked Paris to award the golden apple to the most beautiful of them. In antiquity, the king was judge in all matters. In many instances, however, early disputants selected members of the community as arbitrators, rather than approach the bench. In Iraq, Tulpunnaya was upset with her neighbor Killi for cutting off her water. The arbitrator made Killi give her the equivalent of 10 silver shekels and one ox.[16]

"Equity is justice in that it goes beyond the written law. And it is equitable to prefer arbitration to the law court, for the arbitrator keeps equity in view, whereas the judge looks only to the law...", wrote Aristotle. *The Wasps,* a comic play by Aristophanes, shows an arbitration in which a dog is cross examined. Arbitration survived antiquity, flourished in the Dark Ages, and became a permanent fixture of European culture. From its early roots, the Catholic Church employed arbitration, since the parish priest was often the only educated person, the one the villagers looked up to.[17]

In International Maritime Law, provision was made for a neutral third party to arbitrate disputes on the high seas.

Turning to the North American continent, our original citizens favored ADR. Donna Falahee and Barbara Kennedy provide some excellent research of Native American cultures. Sometime between 1100 and 1500 A.D., the legendary Hiawatha noted that brute power ruled the Iroquois nation. Women and children cowered in fear of their men. Vengeance and bloodlust were the order of the day.

Hiawatha envisioned a replacement for revenge, a longhouse tradition. Five nations, each with its own council fire, would live together in peace as one household. Each family would have its own fireside with its own tools, personal items and clothing, but all families in the longhouse would grow food and hunt as a team, sharing the spoils. When disputes could not be settled locally, the clan chiefs would call a council to settle the matter.

Another noble leader was Dekanawida, the peacemaker. He saw one Great Council comprised of *sachems,* wise men nominated by the clan mothers and females. As long as the women thought the men were doing their job properly, the sachems would continue to hold office. The power, even then, lay behind the throne.

Hiawatha and the Peacemaker envisioned a Great Tree of Peace, standing at the center of the earth, nourished by three double principles:

1. We must work to improve each human being before we can improve the nation.
2. The people must do what is right, but when they do wrong, all parties must receive justice.
3. As a nation, we stand together as one family to protect [from outsiders] what is rightfully ours.[18]

All these principles were implemented by the Iroquois. During Council meetings, only one person could speak at a time. No interruptions were allowed. At the end of a speaker's oration, a short period of silence was observed so that the speaker could add anything he had forgotten. Debates were held to persuade and educate, not as shouting matches. In their desire for peace, the Five Iroquois Nations were always open to see the other side of the issue.

In 1754, Benjamin Franklin spoke of the Iroquois Great Law of Peace at the Albany Plan of Union for the 12 American colonies. Thomas Jefferson studied the Iroquois way. Much of our Constitution is based upon this doctrine. "It should be noted here that the Iroquois Nation provided equality for all people, including women, in the Great Law of Peace," write Falahee and Kennedy. "This is one point that our founding fathers chose not to include in our original governing documents." The Iroquois have followed these ideals and lived in peace for more than 400 years.[19]

The first generation American colonists, for the most part, shunned litigation. They came to this country to obtain land and to escape England, which symbolized corruption and greed. They desired communal peace and harmony. The Puritan code embraced their whole lives — work, social encounters, family relations and spiritual matters. The colonists sensed their obligations to God and to each other. Thus, their "dispute settlement framework was communal, not individual; consensual, not adversarial.[20]

Litigation was difficult and costly. Americans distrusted the English court system. After all, they had fled British rule. The legal profession in America developed slowly, clashing with Puritan values of justice. Society held lawyers in contempt, viewing them as ruthless exploiters who took money from people in their time of need. The attorneys, meanwhile, gradually became rich and entered politics.[21] The seeds of a litigious society had been planted in the New World.

Although many Americans today do not know what ADR stands for, mediation remains the most popular means of settling disputes in some parts of the world. In much of the Orient, litigation is an embarrassing last resort. The Confucian view:

> A lawsuit symbolized disruption of the natural harmony that was thought to exist in human affairs. Law was backed by coercion, and therefore tainted in the eyes of Confucianists. Their view was that the optimum resolution of most disputes was to be achieved not by the exercise of sovereign force but by moral persuasion. Moreover, litigation led to litigiousness and to shameless concern for one's own interest to the detriment of the interests of society.[22]

The Oriental quest for harmony contrasts with Western goals of individual freedom, crystallized in the adversarial system where two attorneys engage in verbal warfare in front of the jury. But the old system, of course, has begun to crack, releasing the phoenix embryo of the ADR paradigm.

We now see neighborhood justice centers in many cities, where volunteers mediate such minor disputes as landlord-tenant, consumer, neighborhood and some criminal issues. Schools, prisons and other institutions are taking part in ADR.

Professional mediation centers process major disputes in divorce and child custody issues, plus conflicts that involve many parties or interest groups. There is much more:

> Many trial and appellate courts, both federal and state, now have programs to mediate settlements — either by judges, magistrates, other court employees or by mediators who are not employed by the courts. Mediation... [also deals with] business disputes of all kinds and with claims against liability insurance companies for damages resulting from personal injuries. In addition, mediation has been used to foster negotiations between farmers and their creditors to avoid foreclosures and in employee grievances and special education and age discrimination disputes...One kind of mediation, known as the Negotiated Investment Strategy (NIS), has been used to help government agencies coordinate policies on a variety of matters from use of land to allocation of funds to social programs.[23]

From the above, we see that mediation is no passing fad but has a rich and deep history in the civilized world. We who are dedicated to this old, yet "new," art of bringing peace to others share a vision that we may create in our world a way for people to resolve their own disputes in healthy, effective ways. This vision is attainable, for it is rooted in a rich, value-laden history, and many people today are becoming receptive to a new level of peace and harmony in their lives.

IN ESSENCE...

- We are in a major paradigm shift from litigation to alternative dispute resolution.

- This new paradigm is based upon talking, co-operation and a win-win attitude.

- The lexicon of dispute resolution must be learned.

- Mediation is effective for just about any type of dispute.

- Mediation has been used in ancient Greece, Rome, Egypt and as far back as Biblical times.

NOTES

1. "Guilty! Too Many Lawyers, Too Much Litigation, Too Much Waste. Business is Starting to Find a Better Way." *Business Week,* April 13, 1992.

2. "Lawyer Jokes," *Nolo News,* Summer, 1993.

3. *Future Edge: Discovering the New Paradigms of Success,* by Joel Arthur Barker (William Morrow and Company, 1992), p.74.

4. "Legal Follies," *Nolo News,* Spring, 1993.

5. Chief Justice Burger's report appears in *Dispute Resolution and Lawyers,* Abridged Edition, by Leonard L. Riskin and James E. Westbrook (West Publishing Co., 1988), pp.8-11.

6. Tevelin is Executive Director of the State Justice Institute, a non-profit corporation established by Congress to award grants to improve the administration of justice in the state courts. For an excellent article by Tevelin, see *NIDR Forum,* Winter, 1992.

7. Jim Dator and Sharon Rodgers' statement from *The Future and the Courts Conference: Alternative Futures for the State Courts of 2020.*

8. *Future Edge: Discovering the New Paradigms of Success,* by Joel Arthur Barker (William Morrow and Company, 1992), p. 39

9. *Rocky Mountain News,* June 14, 1993.

10. *From Conflict to Resolution,* by Susan Heitler, Ph.D. (W.W. Norton & Co., 1990), p. 6.

11. *Getting to Yes,* by Roger Fisher and William Ury (Pendguin Books, 1981), p.4.

12. *From Conflict to Resolution,* by Susan Heitler, Ph.D. (W.W. Norton & Co.,1990), pp.5-6.

13. *Dispute Resolution: Negotiation, Mediation, and Other Processes,* by Stephen B. Goldberg, Frank E. A. Sander, and Nancy H. Rogers (Little, Brown and Co., 1992) p.8

14. "Mediation: 'Nothying Els But Deuidyng By Two,'" by David Singer, in *Arbitration Journal,* September, 1992.

15. "Mediation: 'Nothying Els But Deuidyng By Two,'" by David Singer, in *Arbitration Journal,* September, 1992.

16. *Domke on Commercial Arbitration: The Law of Practice of Commercial Arbitration,* by Martin Domke. Revised Edition by Gabriel M. Wilner (Clark, Boardman, Callaghan, 1990.), Chapter 2, p. 7ff.

17. *Domke on Commerical Arbitration: The Law of Practice of Commercial Arbitration,* by Martin Domke. Revised Edition by Gabriel M. Wilner (Clark, Boardman, Callaghan, 1990.) Chapter 2, p. 7ff.

18. "Historical Roots of Traditional People in Solving Disputes," by Donna Falahee and Barbara Kennedy, 1992.

19. "Historical Roots of Traditional People in Solving Disputes," by Donna Falahee and Barbara Kennedy, 1992.

20. "ADR in Colonial America: A Covenant for Survival," by Susan L. Donegan, in *Arbitration Journal,* June, 1993.

21. "ADR in Colonial America: A Covenant for Survival," by Susan L. Donegan, in *Arbitration Journal,* June, 1993.

22. *Dispute Resolution and Lawyers, Abridged Edition,* by Leonard L. Riskin and James E. Westbrook (West Publishing Co., 1988), p. 83.

23. *Dispute Resolution and Lawyers, Abridged Edition,* by Leonard L. Riskin and James E. Westbrook (West Publishing Co., 1988), pp. 85-86.

PART THREE

Mediation:
A Nuts and Bolts Guide

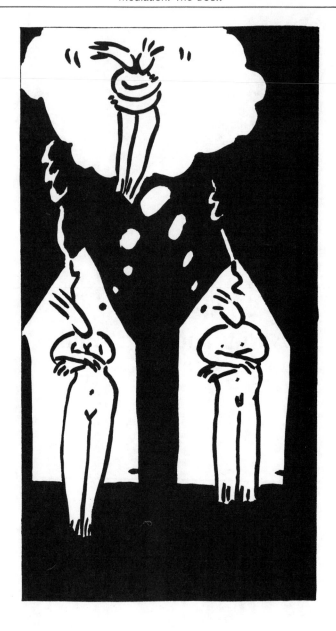

Mediate, Don't Litigate

NINE

What It Takes to be a Mediator

Mediation is
> future focused
> cooperative
> constructive
> creative
> confidential
> win-win
> empowering
> economical
> educational
> transforming
> and a wonderful way to solve problems

A 1992 survey commissioned by the National Institute for Dispute Resolution (NIDR) revealed that eight out of every ten people interviewed who were aware of alternative forms of dispute resolution said that they would likely use an arbitrator or mediator instead of going to court. However, the vast majority of people did not know of any other way of resolving a dispute other than litigation! It is critical that the public be educated about new forms of dispute resolution.

Let us refresh our definition of mediation. Mediation is a dispute resolution mechanism by which parties in a dispute meet with an intermediary who facilitates a settlement of their conflict. A mediator is a neutral third party who assists disputants in resolving their own disputes with the *product* being a final written settlement with which the parties can live. *The mediator is not the decision-maker and cannot impose a settlement.* The mediator actively assists the parties to settle their dispute; the mediator can suggest options for settlement; and the mediator is authorized to terminate the mediation if further efforts appear futile for whatever reasons.

PROFESSIONAL QUALIFICATIONS

What does it take to be a mediator? The Society of Professionals in Dispute Resolution (SPIDR) believes that such performance criteria as neutrality, a demonstrated knowledge of relevant practices and procedures, the ability to listen and understand, and the ability to write well are more useful and appropriate in setting qualifications to practice than the manner in which one achieves those criteria, i.e., formal degrees, training and experience. There is no correlation between mediator competence and formal education.

A set of standards has been developed by SPIDR to assess the potential of prospective dispute resolvers. Here are the standards:

PERFORMANCE-BASED STANDARDS FOR MEDIATORS

I. Skills necessary for competent performance as a neutral include:

A. General

1. The ability to listen actively.

2. The ability to analyze problems, to identify and separate the issues involved, and to frame these issues for resolution or decision making.

3. The ability to use clear, neutral language in speaking and, if written opinions are required, in writing.

4. A sensitivity to strongly felt values of the disputants, in-

cluding gender, ethnic and cultural differences.

5. The ability to deal with complex factual materials.

6. The possession of presence and persistence. One must have an overt commitment to honesty, dignified behavior, respect for the parties, and an ability to create and maintain control of a diverse group of disputants.

7. The ability to identify and separate one's own personal values from issues under consideration.

8. The ability to understand power imbalances.

B. For mediation

1. The ability to understand the negotiating process and the role of advocacy.

2. The ability to earn trust and maintain acceptability.

3. The ability to convert the parties' positions into needs and interests.

4. The ability to screen out non-mediable issues.

5. The ability to help parties invent creative options.

6. The ability to help the parties identify principles and criteria that will guide their decision making.

7. The ability to help parties assess their non-settlement alternatives.

8. The ability to help the parties make their own informed choices.

9. The ability to help parties assess whether their agreement can be implemented.

II. Knowledge of the particular dispute resolution process being used includes:

A. Familiarity with existing standards of practice covering the dispute resolution process.

B. Familiarity with commonly encountered ethical dilemmas.

C. Knowledge of the range of available dispute resolution processes so that, where appropriate, cases can be referred to a more suitable process.

D. Knowledge of the institutional context in which the dispute arose and will be settled.

E. In mediation, knowledge of the process that will be used to resolve the dispute if no agreement is reached, such as judicial or administrative adjudication or arbitration.

F. Where parties' legal rights and remedies are involved, awareness of the legal standards that would be applicable if the case were taken to a court or other legal forum.

G. Adherence to ethical standards.[1]

In Colorado, the Colorado Bar Association and the Colorado Council of Mediators formed a joint committee to study the issue of mediator qualifications. A copy of their report is included as an appendix in this book. It is worth reading.

In the 1988 *Negotiation Journal,* C. Honeyman shares how he tracked five professional mediators on the job. Each had an excellent range of tactics and skills but had distinct personalities. "The Stoic" had extreme patience, "The Bulldozer," had forceful salesmanship, "The Strategist" was able to maintain a balance of self-control, and "The Family Doctor," was able to empathize with all warring factions. The fifth was given the satirical title of "Medicine Show." Perhaps he was a master juggler. The author did not elaborate.

At first glance, no common ground existed between the five professionals:

> ...Three were primarily interested in the problems of the moment and in getting the settlement; two were more concerned with the parties' long-term relationship. One read up on comparable settlements and disputes before going to the meeting; two spent substantial time before each case discussing it with the negotiators on the phone; two others did almost no specific preparation. One mediator routinely used the physical environment, such as whom to sit next to in a caucus; four at least professed to ignore it. Three used sidebar meetings as often as possible; two, as seldom as possible. And, when asked to identify types of cases they particularly liked or disliked, no two came up with the same answer.[2]

Interestingly, all five of these successful mediators followed five specific steps in sequence:

1. INVESTIGATION. Early on, they gleaned hard information from the key disputants, usually in a caucus. Several others noted evasion attempts early on.

2. EMPATHY. Efforts at empathy occurred simultaneously with fact finding, lessening the interrogative aspect of investigation.

3. PERSUASION. Surprisingly, the disputants wanted the mediator to apply pressure on them, as part of the job, for concessions. These skills are similar to that of closing a sale.

4. INVENTION. Early on, if a mediator found a solution to an issue, he or she often kept quiet until well into the session, so as not to appear condescending to the parties. "Let it play itself out," was the operative.

5. DISTRACTION. Friendly talk or jokes, from time to time throughout the negotiations, eased tensions and prevented disputants from locking into their positions.

In 1990 Honeyman added two more skills for effective mediation:

6. MANAGING THE INTERACTION. This is, in plain English, the ability to see the big picture, to distinguish the forest from the trees. The mediator must be effective in developing strategy and managing the mediation process, while keeping a clear head to cope with conflicts that arise in the mediation room.

7. SUBSTANTIVE KNOWLEDGE. This is a controversial point. Must mediators have expertise in the issues involved and the particular type of dispute? Some say, "Master the process and you can handle anything." Or, "You must have expertise in a particular area." And so the debate continues.[2]

The American Arbitration Association looks for a variety of qualities for its panel of mediators:

1. Experience and Competence
2. Neutrality
3. Judicial Capacity and Creativity
4. Reputation and Acceptability
5. Commitment and Availability

PERSONAL CHARACTERISTICS

Most mediation literature lacks in its attention to personal characteristics of the mediator. Over the years, I have noted many styles and approaches of mediators. But the *personhood,* that essential "selfness," is of utmost importance. Several personal qualifications are essential for an adept mediator:

- A good mediator is patient.
- A good mediator is kind.
- A good mediator really cares about people — their feelings, their thoughts, their dreams.
- A good mediator can see people at their ugliest and at the same time experience the goodness within each human being.
- A good mediator is someone who is inclusive, one who can accept a wide variety of people no matter their religion, sexual orientation, gender, race or economic status.
- A good mediator has an excellent sense of humor.
- A good mediator can synthesize all the information that has been put on the table.
- A good mediator can sift through all the garbage and find the treasures hidden within.
- A good mediator is as tenacious as a crab.
- A good mediator is able to write in clear and neutral language.
- A good mediator is an excellent problem solver.
- A good mediator is intellectually bright. He/she must be able to handle cases normally assigned to attorneys and judges.
- A good mediator is able to handle complex human situations.
- A good mediator has common sense.

DIVERSITY OF MEDIATORS

Among mediators there is extraordinary diversity. I have noted several mediation-style polarities: Substance-Focused vs. Process-Focused Mediators; Interventionist vs. Laissez-Faire; and Mediator-Directed vs. Client-Directed. Let's look at each.

Substance-Focused vs. Process-Focused: The Substance-Focused mediator is an expert in the substantive area of the conflict. For example, in an environmental dispute, the mediator may be an expert in water pollution. The Process-Focused mediator is a dispute resolver who is an expert in helping people settle their dispute, no matter what the substance. This latter type focuses on process.

Interventionist vs. Laissez-Faire: The Interventionist mediator strongly directs the unfolding of the negotiations — jumping in to move the process along, keeping communication open, and managing the interaction. The Laissez-Faire mediator is much more laid back and allows the process to unfold with all its twists and turns.

Mediator-Directed vs. Client-Directed: The former has a step-by-step regimen which is applied to each case. The latter is "client driven." The mediation process changes in each context based on the needs, styles and wants of the clients.

On a more humorous note, I have observed several "types" of mediators.

Type A — The Touchy Feely Mediator who encourages everyone to "get it all out" of their system. For this mediator, "communicating" is the ultimate goal, not reaching closure on the dispute.

Type B — The Border Guard Mediator who enforces the rules with a vengeance and shoots anyone who gets out of line.

Type C — The Wise Old Sage Mediator who has resolved 3,122 cases, "just like this," and tells you so. The Wise Old Sage always comes up with the solution before the disputants do!

Type D — The Burned Mediator who was badly hurt in a past relationship and decided to "work out my own stuff" by becoming a mediator.

Type E — The Head-Knocker Mediator who gets a resolution whether the clients want it or not! "You WILL settle."

Type F — The Pollyanna Mediator who, even in the midst of objects flying across the room, keeps saying, "Everything is fine here. Everything will work out."

Type G — The Anal Retentive Mediator who covers every nit-picking detail ad nauseam and then wraps the final agreement in Saran Wrap.

As the reader can see, there are varied perspectives, and indeed conflict, within the mediation field over qualifications and what makes a good mediator. This is part of the excitement and energy in birthing a new profession. Let the dialogue continue.

TEN

Basic Tools for the Journey (Critical Mediator Skills)

It is essential for you as a mediator to have on hand four basic tools of the trade. These tools are critical mediator skills that must be mastered before you venture into the field. They are:

1. Excellent communication skills.

2. The ability to orchestrate movement from positions to interests.

3. The ability to detoxify language.

4. The ability to reframe issues into workable problems which can be solved.

BASIC TOOL # 1: EXCELLENT COMMUNICATION SKILLS

Recently a small ad has been running in a number of national magazines. The headline advertises: "Listening — The Human Ear." Clients dial a number and pay $15 an hour (charged to their credit card) for the opportunity to talk to someone and to be listened to.

Another affliction of our society is the popularity of the 900 telephone numbers. There is now a 900 number that is not a sex or a

Listen/Speak....Speak/Listen

dating line, but a talking line. You call the number and pay $3.69 per minute to speak to a "professional listener" on the other end. People are so hungry for attention that they will pay for synthetic human contact.

When people enter mediation, one of their key needs is to be heard. They want the mediator to listen to them with every ounce of energy. For some, this is the first time in their lives that they have had an audience. M. Scott Peck: "You cannot truly listen to anyone and do anything else at the same time."

In my work, I have developed six fail-safe communication tips:

1) **Validate the essential unconditional worth of each disputant.** When people are in conflict, they tend to feel guilty, ashamed, angry, sometimes out of control, demoralized and put down. You must uncover the humanness of every human being seated in that room. You are observing these people at, possibly, the ugliest moment of their lives. You must transcend this and restore to each disputant his or her inherent dignity. A Quaker friend of mine searches for the "light within" each person.

2) **Encourage each disputant to talk, to open up, by showing that you are interested in the speaker.** Often, in the mediation room, this will be the first time that people sense they can "get their story out there;" that they can tell the tale. In this setting, you must encourage their self-expression by helping them draw out their story. Concentrate intently on what they say. Ask questions. Elicit their story.

Mediation sessions, on the average, run 90 minutes. Except in situations where one party monopolizes or drones on inappropriately, do not cramp your speakers for time. Hear them out fully. Many of our society's ills could be cured if people gave each other the gift of time. Nellie Morton: "Not only a new speech but a new hearing." And as Fred Paddock used to say, "Not just cleaning out the ears but having new ears. Hearing from a new center — the whole body."

3) **Clarify what you are hearing so that you understand the SUBSTANCE of what is being said — the facts, the data — from that individual's perspective.** Take notes. What I do is separate a legal-sized pad into two columns. The left column has the facts — dates, times, places, amounts. This is the substantive grist for the mill. The right side is for the feelings, which will be discussed following this. I go out of my way to interface with each speaker and clarify the details

until I understand. It is my job to grasp the essential facts of each case.

4) Reflect the FEELINGS of the speaker, so that the speaker knows in his or her heart that you are in touch with what is being felt and experienced in the dispute. On the right side of the page I jot down whatever the speaker is feeling, whether it be anger or disappointment or brokenness or whatever. For example:

• Mary is feeling abandoned.

• Roger is afraid his business reputation is being ruined.

The words of Beverly Wildung Harrison are appropriate:

> Feeling is the basic bodily ingredient that mediates our connectedness to the world. When we cannot feel, literally, we lose our connection to the world.
>
> All power, including intellectual power, is rooted in feeling. If feeling is damaged or cut off, our power to image the world and act into it is destroyed and our rationality is impaired. But it is not merely the power to conceive the world that is lost. Our power to value the world gives way as well.

5) Once you understand the substance and the feelings that each speaker is sharing, restate both the substance and the feeling tones of what you are hearing to show that you understand what is being said and to open yourself to correction. "I understand that Jim Osborne, your landlord, owes you three months' back rent." Or, "I sense that you are feeling pretty sad that your wife wants to leave you." This restatement is a reflection of what the speaker has said.

Mediation is not the place where you sit passively and say "Uh huh...uh huh." In the mediation room, the mediator must be engaged. When all the speakers have shared their perspectives, then I summarize out loud all of what has transpired. This summary is a result of the mediator's carefully taken notes. Feelings are included, as well as facts.

As a result of this summary, everyone feels heard. The issues are squarely on the table. Nothing is hidden. In the Agreement to Mediate, outlined further in Chapter 12, I require that the parties agree to full disclosure. Thus, collusion, secret agendas and withholding information are discouraged.

6) Synthesize on an ongoing basis during the mediation the points of common ground, the areas of agreement and the meta-interests which address higher principles such as the public good or the deeper elements that cement a human relationship.

I look at all my notes in front of me, as the mediation progresses, and begin to see where points of agreement come to life as the disputants share their stories. Then such healing words come forth as, "It sounds as if you both have the same interests of John Jr. at heart." Or, "You all want this development project to proceed because it will enhance the economy in this town; but you propose different ways of getting there."

These six communication skills point to one vital fact: the mediator is a mirror in many ways...reflecting back to the disputants what is happening in the mediation room.

BASIC TOOL # 2: THE ABILITY TO ORCHESTRATE MOVEMENT FROM POSITIONS TO INTERESTS

On a cold, winter night, a tiny, emaciated cat was mewing and caterwauling outside my window. She cried for hours and hours. What to do? I could not bring her into the house to be with my two male cats, for she could have been diseased or have been carrying lice and fleas. I went outside and spent two hours with her, stroking and feeding her, and futilely knocking on the doors of my neighbors to see if they would take her in. I finally took her to a 24-hour vet who examined and cleaned the kitten so she could mingle with the other cats.

When I brought her into the house at midnight, all hell broke loose among those cats. The female and the two males began to fight. The boys did not have their claws, but she did. They soon squared off in a rigid, perfectly symmetrical triangle around the food bowls. Each had taken a position. It was a standoff, every cat for himself. But it was more: "I've got to have all the food and all the affection from the humanoids in this house, for if I don't get it, those other cats will take it away from me!" Yet that did not express their true interests underlying their rigid positions. Their interests were to have food, water, warmth, safety and affection.

Human conflict is much like a catfight in which people square off with each other and take positions. The hissing begins. Claws are bared. Mutual interests are ignored and the conflict escalates.

Move from Positions to Interests

A classic account from mediation legend points out the distinction between positions and interests. In the early 1940s, two students were reading in the New York Public Library. The window was open. The sun went down and the coldness of the night chilled their study area.

A conflict ensued. One of the two readers demanded that the window be shut, the other that the window be left open. They complained to the librarian, a wise woman of many years. She sat down and talked to them, discovering that the issue was not whether the window would be open or closed. Rather, one party wanted fresh air and the other refused to be in a draft. The librarian went into a nearby room and opened a different window, thus stopping the draft for the one party and giving fresh air to the other.

THE ICEBERG THEORY

Imagine an iceberg. A large chunk of ice is floating in the frigid sea. Twenty percent of the iceberg is above the water. In dispute resolution, this represents a person's position, i.e., what he or she wants, what that person "must have" in the conflict situation.

As with an iceberg, 80 percent of what the person actually needs is unseen, beneath the water's surface. Forty percent represents personal needs, interests, fears and concerns. On a deeper level in the cold, icy waters, is the other 40 percent which represents a person's meta-interests. These interests are a person's intrinsic leanings toward the greater good, the community, wholeness, toward a higher calling, toward decent relationships and often toward reconciliation. Some examples of meta-interests:

- Stopping the AIDS epidemic which touches everyone.
- Providing equal protection for EVERY citizen per the 14th Amendment of the Constitution.
- Valuing being in community with others.
- Ensuring quality of life for every American.

Even the most despicable combatants possess interests beyond themselves.

The quintessential book on interest-based negotiating is *Getting to Yes* by Roger Fisher and William Ury. The basic thesis of that book is summarized here:

Behind opposed positions lie shared and compatible interests, as well as conflicting ones. We tend to assume that because the other side's positions are opposed to ours, their interests must also be opposed. If we have an interest in defending ourselves, then they must want to attack us. If we have an interest in minimizing the rent, then their interest must be to maximize it. In many negotiations, however, a close examination of the underlying interests will reveal the existence of many more interests that are shared or compatible than ones that are opposed.[3]

Susan Heitler maps the route of three phases of cooperative conflict resolution:[4]

- Expression of initial positions
- Exploration of underlying concerns
- Selection of mutually satisfying solutions

She gives the example of two hungry people, Barbara and Charles. Barbara wants to eat out; Charles wants to eat at home. These are their positions.

Rather than fight it out, Barbara and Charles talk it out, voicing their underlying concerns. Barbara wants something fast, a light meal, wants to eat where it's bright and cheery, and has no desire to cook or wash dishes. Charles doesn't want to dress up for dinner, wants to watch the news on TV, and is ready to make dinner and clean up afterwards.

Aha! They reach mutual solutions. If sandwiches and soup sound good, Charles will provide. Otherwise, Barbara will swing by the grocery store for salad and a barbecued chicken. They eat by the window in their bright kitchen, with the TV news on. Charles does the dishes.

Here is a true story. It happened 10 years ago. A friend was looking for a car. He saw an ad in the newspaper for a Cadillac that the owner was selling for $20. It sounded too good to be true but he decided to follow up. He arranged an appointment, knocked on the door, and a nice-looking lady in her fifties let him in.

She told him it was her car before her husband had died, but as she did not drive very much, the Cadillac had 8,000 miles on it and was in excellent condition. Her asking price remained at $20.

The Iceberg Theory

"What's wrong with the car?" he asked.

"Nothing," she replied.

He took the Cadillac for a test drive. Nothing was wrong.

"Please tell me, what's wrong with the car?" he asked again.

"Nothing," she said.

He bought the Cadillac on the spot and paid her the $20. After she had filled out the pink slip and he had signed it, he pleaded, "What's wrong with the car?"

The woman replied, "My husband wrote in his will that he wanted the proceeds from this car to go to his mistress."

The woman selling the car had one primary interest: to get back at her ex-husband, even in his grave. Oh well, different interests for different folks.

It is imperative that you orchestrate movement from positions to interests *throughout the entire conflict resolution process*. Your task is to get beneath the positions to uncover actual interests.

BASIC TOOL # 3: THE ABILITY TO DETOXIFY LANGUAGE

Usually when disputants enter a conflict situation, they are heated and angry with the world. They use language which reflects those feelings:

"That son of a bitch will never see the children again."

"He is a slum lord, not a landlord, and refuses to fix the plumbing. I will not pay the rent for the past four months."

"Those faggots. All they're doing is destroying the basic moral fabric of this nation."

"That pastor has got to go. He does not preach well, he never makes visits to the hospital, and he simply doesn't care about us."

"Sexual harassment! Why, she has been a tease since she came here."

"I'm keeping the house in this divorce. She has sat on her lazy fat ass and watched Oprah for eight years and never lifted a finger."

"He is the worst doctor on the face of the earth. I knew all along that he was not caring for our son properly."

Now let us take a look at a technique for detoxifying language in highly conflicted situations. The first thing I do as a mediator is to

Neutralize Blame

encourage disputants to use "I" messages. I ask each person to speak for him or herself, to own what he or she is saying, and not to engage in finger-pointing. "I feel angry," NOT, "He screwed me." "I need...," NOT, "You better give me that."

Second, I use statements which help the parties open themselves up to solutions geared toward the future. One technique I use is to ask the disputants to describe the ideal future situation — *after* their dispute is resolved. "What will the ideal outcome look like? Pretend we are sitting here five years from now and tell me how this all worked out."

Third, I steer the disputants from assessing blame on the others. As soon as someone points a finger at you and blames you for something, you are in no mood to settle the conflict or negotiate a settlement. Blame exacerbates the conflict.

Fourth, as a mediator, you need to identify issues objectively, favoring no "side" in the conflict. For example, "How will Mark and Mary Anne share time with Mark, Jr.?" NOT, "When will Mark have visitation?" It is important for you as a mediator to describe the problems as mutual rather than the fault of one party or another. "It sounds as if the two of you have an issue here that needs to be worked out. How can you work together to resolve it?" Another example: Two parents are fighting over custody of their child. Both want time with and access to the child. You might ask, "What kind of schedule can you develop allowing you both to spend time with your son when you will live in two different houses after the divorce:"

Fifth, it is important for you to describe situations in neutral terms rather than judging terms. "It sounds like you're disappointed in the services that your collaborative writer delivered," *not*, "Your writer is an incompetent, lazy inefficient fool."

Sixth, it is important for you to speak in positive, rather than negative, language. Keep the tempo upbeat.

Take a look at the following case.

Jane works as a seasonal employee for the Red Fire Ranger District located on National Forest property in the northern Rockies in Idaho. She is the assistant engine crew boss on a six-person engine crew.

In this part of the country, wildfire is not a major problem. Most fires are small, covering a few acres. They are usually caused by lightning and do not spread fast. Extinguishing fires is not as consuming an activity as are other District functions.

The man Jane works for appreciates her skill as a firefighter and supports her career. She applies for a promotion to a vacant crew boss position at a National Forest in Southern California. In the El Toro Ranger District, many heavy flash fires, which ignite easily and burn quickly, are encountered year-round. Firefighting is top priority.

With her fine record and the support of her supervisor, Jane is selected for the crew boss position at El Toro. She negotiates for and receives housing at the ranger station, usually reserved for married employees. She is selected over and supervises two male employees, Ernest and Willy, who also had applied for the promotion. Her new supervisor is Brad, the fire control officer. He is close to Willy and had wanted him to get the position. But Pam, the ranger, made the final selection. She had no other females on the El Toro Ranger District staff until Jane arrived.

Brad tells Ernest and Willy to clean up and paint the interior of the house, a two-bedroom home that had previously been assigned to a forester, his wife and small child. This was before Jane's insistence on living at the station rather than in town 25 miles away overruled the prior assignment to the family. *Firefighting* is the priority in this unit, so Jane gets first choice.

Jane arrives while Willy and Ernest are finishing the cleaning and painting, and receives a very cool welcome.

After a few days on the job, Jane hears offhand comments from various fire crews and other station employees. "How can a person from Idaho possibly know how to fight fire here?" "How a woman could possibly operate a large tanker truck in these mountains is beyond me...she can't even drive her pickup!"

A few weeks go by. Jane realizes she is being excluded by her peers, a tight-knit group who socialize at the lodge and the lake, and take rafting and fishing trips as well as visits into town on their days off. She also notes that Brad assigns her non-fire assignments and, when fire danger is high, constantly gives her the night shift fire patrol when campgrounds and picnic areas need to be checked around the clock.

Jane finally confronts Brad who quickly informs her that she apparently is not cut out for this District, and that perhaps she should go back to Idaho where the job is easier.

Jane files a complaint based on sex discrimination. Word gets out, and she is totally isolated.

This case was handled by a mediator who did excellent work in detoxifying the situation. Some brief excerpts:

Mediator: "It sounds as if camaraderie and group cohesion are important to both of you. You, Brad, want a competent, ready team here. You, Jane, want to be treated as a valued equal part of the team. It sounds as if you are feeling excluded, Jane. Brad, it sounds as if you need assurance that every employee can and will perform at an acceptable level. As your relationship moves into the future, are you willing to work with me to identify the issues and come to a resolution? I think you can do this."

Notice how this mediator takes away the blaming — using neutral language — identifies issues objectively, states the problem as a mutual one, and is positive in his approach.

BASIC TOOL # 4: THE ABILITY TO REFRAME ISSUES INTO WORKABLE PROBLEMS WHICH CAN BE SOLVED

This is the most important tool for the journey toward a successful resolution. Consider a painting overshadowed by an ugly, chipped frame. Your eye focuses on the ratty frame, not the canvas. This image applies to mediation. The frame is the negative emotions and the toxic language. The painting is the possibility for solution, the opportunity for settlement. The painting gives a picture of the feelings, the data and the needs of the parties. The goal is to keep the essence of the painting, throughout the many twists and turns of the voyage, from initial conflict to final resolution. If the frame becomes tarnished during the journey, the job of the mediator is to position the painting into a new frame, thus, literally *re-framing* it.

The mechanics of reframing entail the reworking of all the information in the conflict into manageable issues which accurately state the problems. These reframed problems are now in a shape which can be worked on and resolved by the parties in the dispute.

The characteristics of good reframing are:

1) The reframing is distilled by the mediator from the perceived needs of all parties. The mediator articulates the issues clearly by focusing on the underlying needs and interests. It is the job of the mediator to pull these submerged needs and interests from the

Reframe

hidden portion of the iceberg and to bring them to light. I term this naming and claiming. You are naming the perceived needs and saying them out loud. Then you are helping the disputants to own or claim their real needs, not just their positions. To accomplish this, the mediator must have concentration and insight. The mediator must focus on and illuminate the underlying needs and interests of the disputing parties. In many cases, the disputants are unaware of these hidden aspects of themselves. The mediator then states out loud the submerged needs and interests of each disputant, which often is a revelation to them. The truth has been revealed, and the stated truth will set them free to move to a resolution.

2) Good reframing does not dwell on the past. It opens up the future and creates an opportunity for settlement. Positions tend to be rooted in past experiences. Interests and needs, once articulated, open us up to new possibilities and new ways of solving problems.

3) Good reframing is stated in neutral and non-toxic language.

4) A good reframe restates inflammatory issues into behavioral terms. "He is an alcoholic and a drug abuser. I never want him around the children after the divorce." Reframed into behavioral terms: "In order for you to be comfortable with Jack being with the children, you would need certain specific guarantees and actions assuring their safety."

5) A good reframe is stated by the mediator so that both parties can "really hear it."

6) A good reframe sets up a framework that is solvable.

7) A good reframe often ends with a question mark. A question mark grammatically opens us up to a solution, to future possibilities, to responding to a question to answer a problem.

Example: A pastor, Reverend Elijah Smith, and the council of Our Shepherd's Church are at odds with each other because the council has not recommended a raise for the pastor in next year's church budget. The pastor was never consulted and has heard about it through the grapevine. He is not so much upset over the lack of a raise as much as his not being a part of the decision.

The reframed statement might be: "How can we as a council and church staff address procedures in the future for making recommendations concerning the pastor's salary in a manner in which everyone is heard?" Note how this reframed statement covers each of the above criteria.

Here are several reframed statements:

- How can we work out this contract dispute so that a strike will be averted and production will not be shut down?
- After the divorce, how will each parent contribute to the financial support of the children?
- What will be the specific terms of this new business relationship?
- How can the needs for economic growth AND protection of the environment be achieved simultaneously?
- What does the supervisor need from the employees, and what do the employees need from the supervisor in order to have a healthy, functioning team?
- Even with one car, what transportation plan can we develop which will allow Mom to get to work and Jonathan to get to practice on time?

Reframed statements must never alter the essential meaning of the original statements. Reframing involves seeing something from a different angle. The impact of reframing is powerful. It literally can change the way the world is seen!

It takes hard work and sweat to become proficient at these four skills. Start using them in your day-to-day life, not just the mediation room. And practice, practice, practice.

Mediator — the Big Ear

ELEVEN

Critical Roles of the Mediator

In the mediation room, the mediator wears a number of hats. These are the eight critical roles of the mediator:

The first is that of *presider*. The mediator must control the process, not the people. The mediator serves in a moderating role over the proceedings.

The second critical role is that of a *calming presence*. People often enter mediation with high levels of emotion. It is critical that the mediator not pour gasoline on the fire, but create a safe space for people by serving as a soothing influence in the room.

The third is that of the *big ear*. When angry people are in conflict, it is next to impossible for them to really hear what they are saying to each other. If they can truly hear what the other disputants are uttering, they probably do not need a mediator! You fulfill an important function as the listening ear for everybody in that room. The information passes through you in such a way that: A) you can hear what is actually being said; and B) you can help the parties listen to one another through you.

The fourth critical role of a mediator is that of *safari guide*. You are leading people on a journey through the deepest, darkest jungles of fears and concerns. At any moment, the Creature from the Black

Lagoon may pop out of the swamp and grab you or any disputant that passes by. You are in charge, as safari guide, to help walk them safely through the thicket and the darkness.

The fifth is that of *archaeologist*. Your job is to dig beneath the positions to discover people's real needs and interests. A five-year-old can help people negotiate, based upon their positions. That is child's play. Your job as a professional mediator is to unearth the hidden treasures.

Fisher and Ury agree that a special knack is required to identify interests, which can be intangible, unexpressed and sometimes inconsistent with positions, which are clear and concrete. You can get the feel of it with two easy exercises.

First, put yourself in the shoes of your client and ask, "Why?" The answer may be a true interest. Why does a landlord fix the rent year by year in a five year lease? To protect himself against rising costs. That is his true interest.

Second, ask, "Why not?" Look at a person's position and ask, "Why didn't you decide to do so and such?" Ask in a spirit of research, of desiring understanding of your client's needs, fears, hopes and desires in the dispute.[5]

The sixth critical role is that of *synthesizer*. Your job is to pull together into coherent form the disparate issues, concerns, facts, data and feelings. You create order out of chaos.

The seventh is the role of *problem-solving coach*. Note: coach, not counselor. This is an important distinction. A coach stands on the sidelines and gives people tips on how to run faster or hit the ball farther. The coach does not go to bat for them. Your role is to stand with them and coach these people through their conflict. You do not impose your ideas upon them but bring about the conditions for the disputants to make their own decisions.

The eighth role of the mediator is as a *dialogue enhancer*. David Bohm and F. David Peat have written a brilliant book, *Science, Order and Creativity*, apropos for when you want to move the disputants from ordinary discussion or debate to real dialogue:

> The term *dialogue* is derived from a Greek word, with *dia* meaning "through" and *logos* signifying "the word." Here "the word" does not refer to mere sounds but to their meaning. So dialogue can be considered as a free flow of meaning

Agent of Reality

between people in communication, in the sense of a stream that flows between banks....

In dialogue, however, a person may prefer a certain position but does not hold to it nonnegotiably. He or she is ready to listen to others with sufficient sympathy and interest to understand the meaning of the other's position properly and is also ready to change his or her point of view if there is good reason to do so....It is not compatible with a spirit that is competitive, contentious or aggressive.[6]

I see Bohm and Peat's concept of "dialogue" as integral to the mediation process. In my surveying the literature, several other authors contribute to understanding the roles and functions of the mediator.

In a passage entitled "The Functions of a Mediator" taken from the book *Dispute Resolution and Lawyers* by Riskin and Westbrook, a celebrated dispute resolver shares his perspective on the heart of mediation:

Lon Fuller, the distinguished professor and arbitrator, described the goal of the mediator in elegant fashion when he wrote: "The central quality of mediation is its capacity to reorient the parties towards each other, not by imposing rules on them, but by helping them to achieve a new and shared perception of their relationship, a perception that will redirect their attitude and dispositions toward one another."[7]

Leonard Riskin, in another passage from the book entitled "Diversity of Mediation Processes," lists the essential roles of the mediator:

– urging participants to agree to talk

– helping participants understand the mediation process

– carrying messages between parties

– helping participants agree upon an agenda

– setting an agenda

– providing a suitable environment for negotiation

– maintaining order

– helping participants understand the problem(s)

– defusing unrealistic expectations
– helping participants develop their own proposals
– helping participants negotiate
– persuading participants to accept a particular solution.[8]

Remember, people are in mediation to bring closure to their dispute, to find a solution to their problems, to reach a final and lasting settlement. Your role as a creative problem-solving facilitator is to help them address all the issues on the table and come to a settlement. Many ideas have been presented. Learn them forwards and backwards — integrate them — so they become part of your cellular makeup. Then you will think clearly and creatively under fire. You will be a seasoned mediator with these concepts plus a few cases under your belt.

TWELVE

A Step-by-Step Method

Recently, a former student of mine, an executive for a large corporation, called me: "Sam, I can't believe it. Your ten-step mediation method works. For the past year I have been applying your methodology to conflict situations within our company, and I have reached a 100 percent settlement rate on every conflict."

This step-by-step mediation model will work for you in the pre-mediation stage, the mediation stage and the post-mediation stage. It is normal to want to jump right in to the negotiating phase. But it is important to work intentionally through each step for a successful mediation. The first stage sets the overall tone for the mediation.

PRE-MEDIATION STAGE

Step One: Contact the clients and their lawyers, if attorneys are involved in the case. Your central task in this first step is to identify the key players. *It is imperative to get every single stakeholder in that dispute to the table.* Otherwise, you have little hope of reaching a final resolution to the problem.

I was asked to mediate the issue of gay and lesbian ordination and appointment in the United Methodist Church. It took months to identify the key players and representatives in that 20-year-old national issue and to bring them to the table. But I knew that if we were not able to identify the pivotal stakeholders and draw them in with the others, a resolution was beyond reach.

During the initial contacts, the disputants may not automatically disclose these important people. Sometimes you must probe. They will emerge as you interview and question each party. This is the same principle used in sales, when you must contact the decision-maker in order to close the deal. It is imperative that you bring together those who have the authority to settle.

One community dispute involved a small town in the throes of a struggle over whether to allow gambling. The mediators chose to convene the entire town. Why? Every resident in that town had a stake in the outcome and legitimately needed a voice. Some 300 people participated in the mediation, which was held in a large Grange hall and was run town-meeting style.

I term those identified as the "client system" and treat them as one unit. Thus, I am not representing or advocating for any individual, but rather I work with the whole.

Your next task in this first step is to collect initial data. The basic facts are required. What are the central issues of this case? What are the documents that need to be presented? The dates? The times? Ask each disputant, usually by phone, to BRIEFLY describe the situation to you.

Another task in Step One is to establish rapport. You must establish a human connection with the disputants during this first stage. Typically, this connection is made over the telephone. It is important that the disputants become comfortable with you and develop a sense of trust.

You also want to give a brief explanation of the mediation process to the disputants so they understand what they are getting into. Be sure to describe the end product to them, namely, a formal, written agreement delineating all the terms which they have negotiated.

The final task of Step One is to schedule the first meeting. This is often a nightmare. You have to juggle numerous calendars with your own, to bring everyone together at the same time in the same place.

Step Two: Establish a creative problem-solving environment. This is an essential component of the pre-mediation stage. Set up the mediation room in a way that creates an atmosphere where people feel safe, comfortable and open. I normally use a round table with chairs of equal height and same design around it. Every person at that table is equal. With a larger group, I suggest a square table or a U-shaped formation. In the room, consider setting a white tablecloth, fresh flowers, coffee, tea and refreshments available for the participants. Place an easel with flip chart and markers at the front of the room.

MEDIATION STAGE

Step Three: Educate the disputants about mediation. You are now in the actual mediation stage. When everyone is comfortably seated, I explain the mediation process. Here is a sample mediator opening statement:

I appreciate your coming here today to mediation. Your presence demonstrates to me that you want to resolve your dispute. The purpose of this session is to work out the issues between you and to come to a full and final resolution.

Let me explain in a step-by-step way how we will proceed so you will know what to expect:

First, each of you will have the chance to explain the situation from your perspective. I want to hear how you view the events which brought you here. I will do my best to understand what you see is going on.

Next, we will identify the specific issues which need to be settled. These issues will create our agenda.

We will work on each issue one by one until resolution is reached. We will work together to see what each of your needs and wants are in order to settle this dispute and meet as many needs as possible. Our goal here is to reach a final solution with which you both can live.

My role is to help you figure out solutions to your problems. I will not make a decision in this case. I will not tell you what to do or judge who is right and who is wrong. YOU will decide what is best in this situation. My job is to facilitate your settlement.

All oral and written communications during the mediation are confidential except (list any and all exceptions to the confidentiality clause you have developed). I will be taking notes but after the mediation I will destroy my notes. In the event that mediation breaks down, I will not testify in any future proceedings regarding this matter.

At any time during the mediation session, you may request a private meeting with the mediator. I call this a one-on-one coaching session. This may be needed if you feel really upset or need to vent your emotions or bounce an idea off me. Everything you say during this one-on-one coaching session will be held in confidence unless you want me to share it with the other party. Each person will be given equal time. Feel free to ask for a coaching session any time you feel the need. I reserve the same right for myself.

I would like to talk about ground rules which help to expedite the mediation process. I ask that you treat one another with respect and dignity in this room. I ask that you not interrupt one another. If you think of something while the other party is speaking, jot it down. You will have a chance to speak later. Now, do either of you have any ground rules which would help us to move toward settlement? (List any and secure agreement.)

Is everyone ready to begin?

Another central task of this third step is for you to establish your role as mediator. You are there to control the process, not the substance or the outcome. You are there to help them negotiate a final settlement with which they can live. You are not making the decision for them. But remember: you are *presiding* at this gathering.

At this point you always want each person in the client system to sign a written mediation agreement. Your agreement may look something like this:

SAMPLE AGREEMENT TO MEDIATE

We, _____ and _____ (names of parties) enter into this Agreement To Mediate on _____ (date) with _____ (name of mediator).

- The client has decided to mediate. The Center for Solutions does not offer legal advice. Each party is hereby advised by the mediator that he/she is encouraged to have any written documents arising out of the mediation (including, but not limited to, any settlement agreement) to be reviewed independently by his/her own counsel prior to signing.

- The Center for Solutions provides a neutral professional who will assist the parties in mediating their settlement and will type all forms, completing documents under the instruction of the client.

- By BACKGROUND, the mediator may be a social worker, psychotherapist, minister, attorney, or from another profession. If your mediator is an attorney by background, he/she will disclose this to you; and he/she is acting as a neutral in this case and cannot and will not represent any party to this action. Mediation is not the practice of law, psychotherapy or counseling. Mediation is the distinct professional practice of alternative dispute resolution.

- The client is entitled to receive information about the mediator's background, training, the duration of the service, and fee structure. The client is encouraged to discuss any aspect of the service.

- In order for this process to be effective, the client understands that open and honest communication is essential. Full disclosure of relevant information is agreed to by the client.

- The client will furnish all information and will make all the decisions with regard to his/her final agreements and be solely responsible for the decisions reached in mediation.

- All written and oral communications, as well as notes taken during the process, will be kept in strict confidence between the mediator and the client, unless:

    1. All parties and the mediator consent in writing to disclose mediation communications.

    2. The communication reveals the intent to commit a felony, inflict bodily harm, or threaten the safety of a child under the age of 18.

    3. The communication is required by statute to be made public.

    4. Disclosure is necessary and relevant to an action alleging willful and wanton misconduct of the mediator or the Center for Solutions, Inc.

- The client agrees not to subpoena or demand the production of any record, notes, work product or the like of the mediator in any legal or administrative proceeding concerning this dispute. To the extent that the client has a right to demand these documents, that right is hereby waived.

- The parties agree that the mediator shall not be called as a witness in any subsequent proceeding in any regard.

- The client intends to continue the service contracted for herein until a satisfactory conclusion is reached. It is understood that any party involved in this process may withdraw at any time. It is agreed that if any party decides to withdraw from the contracted service, the mediator will be contacted and best efforts will be made to discuss this decision in the presence of all parties involved.

- In the event a dispute arises between the mediator and the client(s) arising out of any aspect of the mediation service, the mediator and client(s) agree to enter mediation with an outside neutral third party to resolve their dispute before seeking a resolution in court.

• By our signatures below, we acknowledge and agree
to all the terms listed above.

_____

SIGNATURE   DATE
PRINTED NAME: _____
ADDRESS: _____
PHONE: (DAY) _____ (EVE) _____

_____

SIGNATURE   DATE
PRINTED NAME: _____
ADDRESS: _____
PHONE: (DAY) _____(EVE) _____

_____

SIGNATURE (MEDIATOR)   DATE

The above is only a sample. You will need to develop your own in consultation with an attorney and in accordance with local and state laws, as applicable.

After everyone has signed the Agreement to Mediate, many mediators set ground rules to help the disputants negotiate more effectively. These are the classic ground rules employed by many mediators:

• No interruptions while other people are talking.
• No put-downs, no disparaging remarks.
• No name-calling or blaming allowed in the room.

I prefer only to establish mediation norms as demonstrated in the previously mentioned Mediation Opening Statement and not at this point in the process. I trust people to share and to be open. I think that once you start to set rigid ground rules, people look to you as a cop or as being heavy-handed or overbearing, especially when you are working with people of different cultures. For example, about ten years ago I offended two Asian Americans by suggesting that they not "put one another down," behavior unthinkable to these clients. Disputants may perceive you as putting them down! But if you feel that it is important to have ground rules, you need to be clear about them and set them up front. When using ground rules, customize them to each case.

Step Four: Elicit perspectives. You have laid a strong foundation. Now is the time to roll up your sleeves and begin to mediate the dispute. In step four, you address each party individually. I generally begin with the person who initiated the mediation, asking each in turn to share their perspective:

"What brought you to this mediation? Tell me the nature of this dispute from your point of view. How do you feel about being here? What do you need from this experience? What would the ideal outcome look like? What do you hope for?"

While you elicit this emotional and physical data, be prepared for toxic language. This is when the disputants let down their hair. Summon all your listening powers. Be a sponge. Find out why each party is in the room and each of their positions. But you also must probe deeper to determine their interests, their needs, their concerns, and how they reached these positions. While each person is sharing his or her perspective, you must understand the problems. Ask questions. Draw out information. Allow them to educate you about the dispute.

Remember that each person has his or her own perspective on the dispute. And this perspective IS reality from that person's point of view. In Jane Wagner's *The Search for Signs of Intelligent Life in the Universe*, Lily Tomlin, who plays Trudy, a former creative consultant to multinational corporations and now a bag lady, reflects:

I refuse to be intimidated by
reality anymore.
After all, what is reality anyway? Nothin' but a
collective hunch. My space chums think reality
was once a
primitive method of
crowd control that got out of hand.

In my view, it's absurdity dressed up
in a three-piece business suit.
I made some studies, and
reality is the leading cause of stress amongst those
in touch with it. I can take it in small doses, but as
    a lifestyle
I find it too confining.
It was just too needful;
it expected me to be there for it all the time,
    and with all
I have to do —
I had to let something go."[9]

We all have read the story of the three little pigs and the big bad wolf. Realize that this book was written from the point of view of the swine. Have we heard the wolf's side of the story?

The job of the mediator is to understand each disputant's reality and the issues needing resolution. While writing this section, I saw a bumper sticker: DON'T MESS WITH MY REALITY!

Bohm and Peat are helpful at this point:

> What is needed is for each person to be able to hold several points of view, in a sort of active suspension, while treating the ideas of others with something of the care and attention that are given to his or her own. Each participant is not called on to accept or reject particular points of view; rather he or she should attempt to come to an understanding of what they mean. In this way it may be possible to hold a number of different approaches together in the mind with almost equal energy and interest....It is our suggestion that out of this freely moving dialogue can emerge something that is creatively new, for example, the perception of a new link or metaphor between very different points of view...
>
> What is essential here is the presence of the spirit of dialogue, which is, in short, the ability to hold many points of view in suspension, along with a primary interest in the creation of a common meaning.[10]

Separate Personalities from Problems

Step Five: Set the agenda. Your job as a mediator is to take all this information you have heard and to create joint workable problem questions. You need to develop a set of agenda items that need to be resolved in this given case. Stand in front of the client system and write these issues on a flip chart so all can see them clearly. You may have two items; you may have twenty, depending on the complexity of the case. You want a visual agenda that outlines each issue that needs resolving. You will need to rely on all the skills we have talked about earlier — detoxifying, reframing — to create a solid agenda. Your central job here is to write up the issues as joint workable problem questions.

A visual presentation of the issues to be resolved sets them in concrete terms, in black and white. When a problem is nebulous, unformed and murky, it lurks in the realm of the unknown, in Black Lagoon territory. When it is block-printed on a large flip chart in concise, detoxified language, that same problem has risen out of the swamp into the land of the known. It is "graspable," hence solvable.

People tend to scratch their heads and look down at their feet when pondering the imponderable. The physical act of looking up at a flip chart makes them raise their heads which, by definition, is forward directed, future oriented, *uplifting*. For the first time, all the disputants will be concentrating on the same visual point on the flip chart and, therefore, starting to work together towards solving the issues.

Here are some sample agenda items written as Joint Workable Problem Questions:

- What step-by-step system for resolving future disputes can we develop in this organization?
- After the divorce, how shall we ensure that both John and Mary will maintain a similar standard of living as they currently enjoy?
- In order to avert the cost of bankruptcy, what terms can the farmer and lender agree to in order to each get what they need?
- How can Sally's mother be assured that she is safe on dates, and at the same time Sally be emancipated from her mother?

A solid agenda item has several characteristics:
- It is future-oriented.
- It is based on the interests of each party.
- It is open-ended.
- It is solvable.
- It ends in a question mark.

Step Six: Gather data that is needed to solve each of the agenda issues. Take each issue and either collect the information right there on the spot or assign homework. One of the issues may state: "After our divorce, how will we both meet the financial needs of our children?" You then might ask the divorcing couple to go home to prepare a financial statement and a realistic budget for raising the children after the divorce.

Step Six often entails leaving the session and getting more information from a variety of sources. People can go away and gather the information that they need in order to bring it back to the table so they can make an informed decision.

Step Seven: Enter the problem-solving phase of the mediation process. Now and only now are you ready to problem solve. It is your task at this point to facilitate the resolution of each agenda item one by one.

This step may appear as the crux of the mediation process. I do not agree. Every aspect is equally important. Until the groundwork is laid and all the steps have been worked through to this point, resolution will not come easily. Careful preparation marks the difference between an amateur and a true professional. Mediation is no exception.

The central task of the seventh mediation step is to assist the parties to negotiate a settlement. Always remember: *They are doing the negotiating; you are doing the assisting.*

In *Getting to Yes,* Fisher and Ury offer several useful tips:

Always separate the people from the problem. In conflict situations, people tend to get personalities muddled with the issues. That is normal human behavior. You, the mediator, are to keep the issues separated from the personalities. Be tenacious about staying on track.

"I told you...he is a slumlord and never fixes the plumbing." You will reframe the comment and say, "It sounds like the issue is how to get the plumbing in your apartment building repaired as quickly as possible."

Focus on interests, not positions. "I told you he's a slumlord and he never fixes the plumbing. So I'm not going to pay for the past three months' rent." Not paying rent is the position. But the underlying interest is to get the plumbing fixed.

You, the mediator: "I hear you say what your position is — you're not going to pay. But it sounds to me what you really want out of this is plumbing that works."

Invent options for mutual gain. In that same vignette, you say, "How can you, Mrs. Magillicote, get your plumbing repaired, and at the same time, Mr. Pototski, how can you get the money that you're owed?" You are inviting options for mutual gain.

Insist on using objective criteria. For example, turn to the blue book value of a used car rather than haggling over the price. Get a property appraised to determine its value. This will save wear and tear on your brain.

Know your Best Alternative to a Negotiated Agreement (BATNA). Before you decide to buy that Ford coupe from your neighbor for $6,000, check how much a similar car would cost you elsewhere. That is your BATNA. Find out the other party's BATNA as well. What would your neighbor get for the car if she sold it elsewhere?[11]

I share here some of my tips during this problem-solving phase:

- Continue to listen with focus.
- Help people move from their positions to get in touch with their real interests.
- Coach them to negotiate out of their interests, not their positions.
- Encourage give and take.
- Earnestly seek common ground. When anybody offers any overlap of any agreement, I see it as a gift. I claim it. I grab it.
- Brainstorm possible solutions. Try to generate creative ways in which these people can get out of their predicament. Sometimes I will even throw in a possible solution.

But I only do this after they have come up with at least two possibilities.

Fisher and Ury explore the art of brainstorming:

> To invent creative options, then, you will need (1) to separate the act of inventing options from the act of judging them; (2) to broaden the options on the table rather than look for a single answer; (3) to search for mutual gains; and (4) to invent ways of making their decisions easy.[12]

• Model and reinforce mutual problem solving.

In the mediation room I sometimes wear a button that says: "Agent of Reality." If people get too far out in left field, I will call them on it. I gently (and sometimes not so gently) bring them back to earth. It also is appropriate to have them bounce their ideas off other professionals (such as attorneys, child development specialists, CPAs, etc.) to test reality.

A couple is married three years. Both are in their early 30s. Each makes $20,000 a year. They seek a divorce. The woman wants alimony of $1,000 a month until she retires. Her chances of getting this are probably unrealistic in any court of law in this country.

I try to raise doubts. I ask her things like, "OK, if you can't settle this here, if you cannot come to a solution, do you think you would get that kind of settlement in court?" An Agent of Reality...that's what you are. Important note: I only raise doubts in the coaching sessions so as not to embarrass or undermine the parties in front of each other.

At the conclusion of our seventh step, the agreement has been made *orally* to the satisfaction of all parties. You state the terms out loud, reading from your notes. The session is over, and they leave.

A few moments of reflection on the art of problem solving:

> Don't be afraid to explore;
> > Without exploration there are no discoveries.
> Don't be afraid of partial solutions;
> > Without the tentative there is no
> > accomplishment.
>
> — Deng Ming-Dao[13]

Step Eight: Prepare the written agreement. The central task for this step is to finalize the terms of the settlement in a written document. It is vitally essential to put the settlement in writing. It honors the work that people have done. You now prepare in a final written form all the agreements your clients have made. Strive to use language that is balanced and neutral. Citibank once had a default agreement written by lawyers which had 304 words of gobbledygook. The same clause was later reduced to 31 words. *Think clarity and simplicity.* Clearly and succinctly cover every agreement.

All good writing is concise. Most people have bad habits they need to break. Here are a few hints:

- Pretend your readers are 12 years old. Albert Einstein said, "Everything should be made as simple as possible, but not simpler."
- Remove your specialist's hat. Eliminate the unnecessary.
- Do not try to impress your audience. Communicate, don't alienate.
- Beware of polysyllabic words. Some necessary technical words — fair enough. But go for simplicity.
- Get rid of vague words such as *it* and *there*. Change "It was agreed that Mark will pay Bill," to "By June 1, 1994, Mark will pay Bill $250."
- Read your finished document carefully before sending it out into the world.

The written agreement is crucial. A well-written agreement assures that the settlement terms will be met by all parties. This document carves in stone the decisions, intentions and future actions of the participants, hammered out by the disputants and the mediator. It is not a judgment handed down from on high.

Why is mediation so successful? There is no District Attorney, no court system, no jail to serve as threats. True, these loom as deterrents if settlement cannot be reached. But one of the big reasons mediation is workable in the dispute resolution field is the psychological effect of the written agreement. People own solutions which they have crafted and committed to paper. Several elements go into a well-written agreement:

Avoid legal terminology. Many people are tired of the legal game. They want to take responsibility for their own disputes. Thus, when you craft the written agreement, stay away from legalese. Use "bring about" instead of "effectuate;" "inform" instead of "apprise." "Write" or "telephone" is better than "communicate." Steer clear of, "Parties of the first part hereby stipulate that the party of the second part will hereto…"

Avoid formalities when identifying people in the agreement. Use first and last names — John Evans and Susan McCarthy — instead of Mr. Evans and Ms. McCarthy, or "the Claimant" and "the Respondent." *Use the real names of the parties.*

DON'T SAY: The Respondent furniture store will let the Claimant exchange his loveseat…

SAY: Empire Valley Furniture Emporium, Inc., will allow James Turner to exchange…

State specific dates in the agreement.

DON'T SAY: The respondent, Constance Wallis, agrees to remove the battered house trailer from her backyard as soon as possible.

SAY: Constance Wallis will remove the house trailer from her backyard by May 10, 1994.

Spell out money transactions. Leave nothing to chance.

DON'T SAY: Herbert Presley agrees to pay Tom Maloney the sum of 628 dollars.

SAY: Herbert Presley will pay Tom Maloney 628 dollars by certified bank check or money order sent by U.S. mail to Mr. Richardson at 866 Spring Ave., Northhampton, Massachusetts, by June 9, 1994.

Do not mention whose fault it is. This saves face among the parties and helps them to move forward. If the landlord has agreed to fix the heating unit, let the agreement read:

Allan Knight, manager of Desert View Apartments, agrees to repair by 5 P.M., October 3, 1994, the heating and air conditioning unit of Apartment 6, occupied by Charles Downing.

Make the agreement reflect future contingencies, if possible. If one of the disputants reneges on his or her part of the agreement, note that the other may bring the offending party back to mediation or seek relief in court.

EXAMPLE: (who) Empire Valley Furniture Emporium, Inc., will

allow James Turner (what) to exchange his Olsen green loveseat, Model 340, for any piece of furniture currently in stock of equal or lesser value. The exchange can be made (when) during regular business hours until April 30, 1994, (where) at Empire Valley's Westside Branch, 336 Acoma Avenue, Banning, California. (how) Empire Valley's store manager, Mr. James Callahan, will make himself available to accommodate the exchange.

The agreement will probably spell out certain actions of each disputant. To avoid confusion, list each requirement separately and number it.

EXAMPLE: The Cotters and Jacksons, neighbors of five years, have come to the following agreement:

1) Jeff and Sally Cotter agree to keep their dog, Rufus, in side their home after 8:00 P.M.

2) Paul and Nancy Jackson agree not to interact with the dog in any manner (no teasing, no yelling, no throwing objects).

3) If a dispute arises in the future between the Cotters and Jacksons, they agree to first call one another on the phone to try to work it out prior to calling the police. A complete sample agreement is found in the Appendix section of this book.

Step Nine: Enter the closure phase. You meet again with the parties in the mediation room and present to them the final completed document. Together you review for accuracy the written agreement. You say, "If I have made an error or you would like to change something, please say so." You revise the agreement on the spot, if possible.

In the mediation room, it is ideal to keep a word processor and a printer to make these final changes. Our mediators at the Center for Solutions always do their own agreement preparation. We have found this easier than to use secretaries.

You then secure a commitment from your clients to act upon the agreement. To quote Guillaluhme:

"Come to the edge," he said. They said, "We are afraid."
"Come to the edge," he said. They came. He pushed them and they flew.

Your clients will have the final agreement in hand when they leave. Parties may take the agreement directly to court (if the court is involved); or, more typically, they will show it to their attorneys for document review. If an attorney sees a problem or if a client needs to renegotiate a fine point, the parties can come back for further mediation. I encourage my clients to take the agreement and sign it in the presence of a Notary Public — not in my presence. Once an agreement is signed, an enforceable contract has been entered.

In 95 percent of the cases I mediate, complete resolution is reached. What happens to the other five percent? When no resolution is achieved through mediation, you need to discuss with your clients the possible alternatives for getting their dispute resolved. To abandon them at this point would be irresponsible and, I believe, unethical.

Spend some time talking it over with them. "Would you like to have it arbitrated, where an arbitrator as a neutral third party will render a decision? Do you want to take it to court...or do you just want to drop the whole thing? (That happens sometimes.) Now...what are you going to do if you can't resolve this problem?"

POST-MEDIATION STAGE

Step Ten: Follow up. This is the post-mediation stage. Within two weeks after mediation, I call the principals who were involved in the dispute and obtain an evaluation from them. "How are you doing since we finished the mediation? What did I do that was helpful to you as a mediator? What could I have done that would have been more helpful? Can I be of further service?"

Most people will honor the final document. In terms of the implementation of the agreement, I experience a 98 percent compliance rate. Why? The people have created the agreement themselves. They claim high ownership of it. It was not imposed on them. If again some clause needs fine tuning, I always keep the door open and encourage the disputants to come back to mediate with me. If mediation does not work out, they can move on to a "higher" dispute resolution forum. And that's all right.

I have a friend in Boulder who is an excellent mediator, one of the best in the country. She has mediated with a number of families who are in highly conflicted divorce situations. They have so much dissension in their post-divorce relationships that they still need a mediator to work with them every couple of months to negotiate ongoing issues — typically around the children. My friend has become like the family doctor. Her clients call her and say, "We're having a conflict." They come in to her office and she mediates the dispute on the spot.

The step-by-step mediation model presented in this section is a template for you to use. Modify it. Customize it. Personalize it to your style. And make it your own.

THIRTEEN

Special Strategies for Moving the Parties toward Settlement

Four strategies may be employed by you to help move people toward resolution of the issues that are on the table. The first technique is the **one-on-one coaching session.** Many mediators call this a caucus. I still think of a bunch of cigar-smoking politicians in a closet when I hear "caucus."

Here, the mediator will meet privately with every disputant in the case. The mediator remains in the mediation room with the person being coached while the others go to the waiting room.

This private session is optional. In many mediations, the flow of the negotiation is going so well that there is no reason to call for one. Understand that a party may request a coaching session anytime during the mediation. You may also call for the same. All parties must honor anyone's request for a one-on-one coaching session. In order to be fair and equitable, whenever the mediator has a private session with one party, the other party must be offered a session.

Why do we use these coaching sessions? First, to break deadlocks. When the parties become so entrenched in their positions that the mediation is not moving forward, this is an appropriate time to call for a coaching session.

In their divorce case, Roberta Gantz repeatedly says: "I want sole custody of the two children!" Jonathan Gantz keeps saying: "*I* want sole custody of the two children." They have reached deadlock. You need to call for a one-on-one coaching session with each party. You probe to find out what is going on underneath these ultimatums, to flush out their real interests and wants, and learn why they cling so tightly to their respective positions. Often they will not reveal these more personal issues in the mediation session but will tell you in private.

A second purpose for relying on one-on-one coaching sessions is to diffuse volatility. When emotions are running so high in the room that you are unable to detoxify them, timing is of the essence. Do not wait until the agitation level has escalated to the degree that it jeopardizes the entire mediation. Many mediators wait too long to call for time out. You need to follow your gut-level instincts. As a mediator, you have the responsibility to ask for a coaching session before the volcano erupts.

Third, sometimes you perceive that you are not getting all the information in the group meetings, that someone is holding back. Call for a coaching session. Ask questions. Probe. You may just find the missing link.

A fourth reason to hold a one-on-one coaching session is to confront a disputant's fantasies with reality. This is the time to do reality testing with a client in private.

Morton L. Smith, M.D., allegedly has performed medical malpractice on Susan Roquette's right knee. The case has come to you to mediate. Ms. Roquette wants $500,000. In a court of law, the case is worth $25,000 at best — according to attorneys for each side! It is time to match Susan's desires with reality, to engage in serious reality testing. This should not be done in front of Doctor Smith, for it would likely humiliate or hurt the feelings of the patient, as well as damage her case.

In a private session, you look the person in the eye and say, "What do you really think this is worth? What would you get if you took this to court? Have you discussed this with your attorney?"

Recently, I saw a wonderful play, *The Night Larry Kramer Kissed Me.* I remember one line: "The truth will set you free...but first it will piss you off." This often happens in the coaching session when dealing with reality.

A fifth motivation for calling a private session with a client is when a gross imbalance of power exists in the mediation room. When you see one party verbally beating up on the other, STOP the mediation. It is going nowhere. Before continuing, you need to speak with all the disputants to determine if they can negotiate out of a sense of parity.

Stanley Milquetoast, a clerical office worker, is in a salary dispute with his administrator, Charles E. Willoughby. During mediation, Willoughby on two occasions threatens to fire Milquetoast if he continues to press him in the dispute. Milquetoast withers. You immediately call time out separately for both parties.

Coaching session A with boss:

MEDIATOR TO BOSS: "With the tactic you are using, Mr. Willoughby, do you think you can resolve this dispute? Will threatening to fire Mr. Milquetoast get you what you need?"

BOSS: "It wasn't my idea to go into mediation. I'm just going along with it, but I'm getting angrier and angrier at the way Mr. Milquetoast is accusing me of paying him less than he deserves. As far as I'm concerned, he is worth a big fat zero, and I wish I'd gotten rid of him a long time ago...but actually, I don't want him to quit."

Coaching session B with employee:

MEDIATOR TO EMPLOYEE: "It seems like you're really feeling intimidated, that you feel powerless in this situation. What do you need in this mediation?"

EMPLOYEE: "I need a reassurance from my boss that I will not be terminated if I state my point of view."

MEDIATOR: "When we reconvene in the mediation session, are you willing to put that on the table? Or would you like for me to explain it to the other party on your behalf?"

EMPLOYEE: "The latter, please. I just cannot afford to lose my job at this time, regardless of the low salary I am getting. My wife has lung cancer and the hospital bills are horrendous. I do not know how you would handle it, but I'm not willing to lose my job over this dispute."

MEDIATOR: "So it is really important that you get assurance from your boss that you won't get fired over this issue of salary."

EMPLOYEE: "Yes. That's right."

MEDIATOR: "All right. I will meet again with Mr. Willoughby privately before we continue the joint meeting."

A sixth reason for calling these private sessions is to build rapport with the client. If you are not developing a trusting relationship with the disputants, it is time to stop the process and hold a one-on-one coaching session. Find out from the disputants how they are feeling about the mediation process, if they are pleased with your style of mediation, and so on.

In my experience, 40 to 50 percent of the cases require coaching sessions. Feel free to use this special strategy to expedite the mediation process.

The second special strategy for moving clients toward settlement is **mirroring**. You as a mediator are a mirror for the disputants. Your objective is to mirror back to them what they are saying, what they are feeling, what they are wanting, and what they are needing in this situation. Often, unknown to you, this may be the first time during the dispute that they have had the chance to "put it all out there." You, as mirror, reflect back everything they are saying and sharing.

If a disputant pounds his fist on the table like Khrushchev and raises his voice two octaves, you do not mirror in kind. You say, "By the pounding of your fist, it seems to me that you are angry." This is *mediator mirroring*, not absolute mirroring.

In terms of mediator mirroring, there are three statements that you will want to remember.

1) "So what you are saying is..." This has to do with reflecting the facts, the data, the substance.

2) "So what you are feeling is..." This has to do with the feeling tones, the experience of the individual.

3) "So what you are needing in this situation is..." This must be anchored in the client's underlying needs and interests.

Mirroring

Let Out the R.A.T.S.

Mirroring is used throughout the step-by-step mediation process discussed earlier, from the very first contact until the post-mediation follow-up. This mirroring technique leads the mediator along the journey of discovery into the deeper core issues of the dispute and to a deeper appreciation for the people involved. Without this ability to understand the human condition, to ascertain the underlying needs and interests of every single person in the mediation room, the mediator degenerates into a second-rate talk show host.

Bohm and Peat elucidate the goal of mirroring:

> ...In any case, the truly wise individual is one who understands that there may be something important to be learned from any other human being.
>
> ...the essential need is for a "loosening" of rigidly held intellectual content in the tacit infrastructure of consciousness, along with a "melting" of the "hardness of the heart" on the side of feeling. The "melting" on the emotional side could perhaps be called the beginning of genuine love, while the "loosening" of thought is the beginning of awakening of creative intelligence. The two necessarily go together. Thus, to be "warmhearted" and "generous" while keeping ideas rigid will lead only to frustration in the long run, as will intellectual clarity that is allied with cold hardheartedness.[14]

A third special technique for moving disputants towards settlement is letting out the R.A.T.S., an acronym for **Realistic Alternatives To Settlement.** When you let out the R.A.T.S., you want to engage people to find out what they plan to do if they cannot settle their dispute in this mediation room. You always need to put the responsibility back on the client.

"Do you want to mediate this dispute? Do you want to settle this here? In your heart of hearts, do you truly desire to settle this dispute? Would you rather settle it in some other forum? Do you want to take it to court? Go into arbitration? Do you want to live with the problem? Do you want to drop the whole thing? Where do you think you will get your best deal...in this room or through one of these alternatives?"

Play the What If Game

Sometimes I will spell out the costs of taking a case to court. Sometimes I will just challenge the disputants to find out for themselves. Often I will encourage them to discuss the alternatives with their attorneys.

When you bring up the alternatives, the R.A.T.S., most disputants would rather mediate a settlement.

The fourth special strategy for moving parties toward settlement is to play the **"What If"** game. The "What If" game involves your raising questions about the viability of the settlement to which they are aspiring. You ask questions that may create doubts in the client's mind. These questions sometimes anticipate what will happen in the future if, for instance, one of the parties breaks the agreement. It is a worst case scenario game.

The stalwarts of the Lily of the Valley Church of God think their pastor has gone a little off the deep end, leaning toward a Born Again approach. Some of the new church members welcome his tent-preaching style. The church council, comprised of the old diehards, are in an intensive mediation session with the pastor. They want to get rid of him. He digs in his heels and refuses to change or submit his resignation. You dangle the R.A.T.S. in front of them. They choose to hang in and mediate. So you try the "What If" game.

MEDIATOR: What if you cannot resolve this dispute within the parish?

COUNCIL MEMBER #1: Well, we could get a reputation as being a "problem church."

COUNCIL MEMBER #2: We could get a bad name in the community.

COUNCIL MEMBER #3: This could become a place where no pastor would ever want to come again.

MEDIATOR (to pastor): And you, sir, what would happen to you if this dispute is not resolved?

PASTOR: I'm afraid that with this history of conflict, I'd have trouble getting a good job in another church.

It is important to remember that these four techniques are useful in moving people through the mediation process. Please note that they are not sequential. Any of these special strategies may be used at any stage of the mediation process, with the goal being to move the negotiations along. Keep these different techniques in your skill bank to pull out and use when needed.

IN ESSENCE...

• Basic mediation tools include excellent communication skills, the ability to move the parties from positions to interests, the skill to detoxify language and the ability to reframe.

• The seven critical roles of the mediator in the mediation room are: presider, calming presence, the big ear, safari guide, archaeologist, synthesizer and problem-solving coach.

• The ten steps to conflict resolution:
   1) Identify the key players.
   2) Set up a problem-solving environment.
   3) Educate the disputants.
   4) Elicit perspectives.
   5) Set the agenda.
   6) Gather more data.
   7) Enter the problem-solving phase.
   8) Prepare the written agreement.
   9) Enter the closure phase.
   10) Prepare the follow-up.

• Four strategies to nudge the parties toward resolution are:
   1) Coach them one-on-one.
   2) Mirror their feelings and statements in a positive way.
   3) Release the R.A.T.S.
   4) Play the "What If" game.

NOTES

1. Excerpted from "The Report of the SPIDR Commission on Qualifications," reprinted in the May, 1989, *Dispute Resolution Forum,* NIDR, Washington, D.C.

2. "Five elements of Mediation," by C. Honeyman, first appeared in *Negotiation Journal,* 1988. Excerpts here taken from *Dispute Resolution: Negotiation, Mediation, and Other Processes,* by Stephen B. Goldbert, Frank E. A. Sander and Nancy H. Rogers (Little, Brown and Co., 1992), pp. 113-116.

3. *Getting to Yes,* by Roger Fisher and William Ury (Penguin Books, 1981), p. 43

4. *From Conflict to Resolution,* by Susan Heitler, Ph.D. (W. W. Norton & Company, 1990), p. 22ff

5. *Getting to Yes,* by Roger Fisher and William Ury (Penguin Books, 1981), p. 45.

6. *Science, Order and Creativity,* by David Bohm and F. David Peat (Bantam Books, 1987), p. 241.

7. *Dispute Resolution and Lawyers, Abridged Edition,* by Leonard L. Riskin and James E. Westbrook (West Publishing Co., 1988), p. 95.

8. *Dispute Resolution and Lawyers, Abridged Edition,* by Leonard L. Riskin and James E. Westbrook (West Publishing Co., 1988), p. 92.

9. Lily Tomlin performing as Trudy in the one-woman play, *The Search for Signs of Intelligent Life in the Universe,* by Jane Wagner (Harper & Row, 1985).

10. *Science, Order and Creativity,* by David Bohm and F. David Peat (Bantam Books, 1987), pp. 86-7, 247.

11. Excerpts from Fisher and Ury's book, *Getting to Yes,* appear in *Dispute Resolution: Negotiation, Mediation, and Other Processes, Second Edition,* by Stephen B. Goldberg, Frank E. A. Sander, and Nancy H. Rogers (Little, Brown and Co., 1992), pp. 36-37.

12. *Getting to Yes,* by Roger Fisher and William Ury (Penguin Books, 1981.), p. 62.

13. *Daily Meditations,* by Deng Ming-Dao (Harper-Collins, 1992).

14. *Science, Order and Creativity,* by David Bohm and F. David Peat (Bantam Books, 1987), pp. 270-271.

PART FOUR

Setting Up a Mediation Practice

Launch Your Ship

FOURTEEN

Benefits and Rewards

MAKING A LIVING

Let me say at the outset that when you are beginning a private mediation practice, for the first two to three years you will probably not be able to make a living. While you gradually become known in the community as an exponent of this relatively new field, it is important not to give up your current source of income. *Keep your day job!* Think of mediation as an ancillary profession. If you are already an attorney, as many mediators are, start a mediation practice on the side. If you are a social worker, keep your social work practice as a safety net. If you are an MBA, stay with your company.

Down the road, an individual can make a moderate living as a professional mediator in private practice. A reasonable annual income to expect for an experienced mediator ranges from $30,000 to $70,000.

GETTING YOUR FOOT IN THE DOOR

Your first step is to attend a quality mediation training program. This is a must. The industry standard is 32 to 40 clock hours for basic training. Educational sessions are held across the country. A good mediation training course includes lectures, experiential exercises and hands-on role playing. If you do not know where training courses are held, write the Institute for Mediation and Arbitration Training, Inc., 50 S. Steele St., Suite 222, Denver, Colorado 80209-2807, or call 1-800-995-1985, and leave your name, address, and daytime and evening phone numbers.

Occasionally a mediation position will be made available through local, state or federal agencies. If you can secure one of those, this is a viable option. Your main objective is to gain experience in mediation while continuing to earn a decent living.

Many large metropolitan areas and medium-sized cities will have a community or public mediation center which typically resolves neighbor/neighbor disputes, roommate disputes, simple contract disputes, consumer disputes, etc. Many of these places need volunteers. Look in the Yellow Pages under "Mediation Centers" or call your local Bar Association and inquire about community mediation programs in your geographical area. Contact these organizations directly to volunteer to be a mediator.

If you happen to reside where there is no public mediation center, contact a private mediation firm and inquire if it has an internship program. The Center for Solutions in its Colorado operation, offers an internship program specifically designed for working adults who want to be mediators. It is a seven-month program, requiring about five or six hours a week, allowing you to continue your regular profession. The program offers hands-on work with clients, co-mediation with an experienced mediator, continuous supervision, case conferences and ongoing training.

If you live in a rural area where there are no mediation facilities, do not despair or engage in an expensive relocation. Over the years I have worked with several students who contracted with me for long distance consultation. They pay me to supervise them over the phone. They start a practice and have their own clients. Then I or another experienced mediator offer *shadow consultations* between sessions.

I find that it takes about 10 cases for a beginning mediator under consultation with an experienced mediator to reach an acceptable level of competence. You can do this by long distance or in person. Thereafter, your expertise will evolve from the many conflict situations that come your way. In the not too distant future, you may offer consultation to the next generation of mediators.

The Center for Solutions, with which I am affiliated, is based in Colorado and Southern California. It is a private dispute resolution firm which offers mediation, arbitration, mediation/arbitration (med/arb) and consulting. As our firm has done, you might wish to consider offering several ADR methodologies in addition to mediation.

If you truly want to be a mediator, nothing will stop you. Only your own mental limitations can get in the way. The market is limitless. Private mediation firms can be found in most major cities across the U.S. and Canada. Yet there is so much room for expansion. Anywhere humans live together, from Skagway, Alaska, to the bayous of Louisiana, there will be disputes. Educate people to the benefits of mediation over costly litigation, and you are in business.

INTRINSIC BENEFITS OF MEDIATION

Apart from a comfortable living, mediation offers a number of intrinsic benefits. First, you experience a high satisfaction rate derived from helping people work out their differences. Most of you have read corporate studies showing that job satisfaction is more important to employees than a higher salary. Think on that as you weigh your options.

Second, you see people at critical junctures in their lives — when they are really hurting or broken or angry — and thus you are privileged to interface with them at meaningful moments in their lives. So many professions demand loyalty to a product that contributes to the malaise of our already weary planet. The profession of mediation presents remedies, not headaches.

Third, you are involved in helping people solve problems, a creative, energizing and challenging activity. You sow the seed and trust the promise. Your clients seize upon new opportunities. You are the architect of their own happiness.

Fourth, it is just plain *fun* to be involved in watching people come to solutions they can live with. You will be part of the fortunate few who look forward to Monday mornings.

Fifth, you get that certain glow, knowing that you are empowering individuals to do what is best in their own lives rather than allow a system to impose judgments upon them. Remember, in a courtroom one team wins and the other loses. Same as in sports. Some weep, others laugh. At the conclusion of a mediation, everyone emerges strong, imbued with respect for themselves as well as the other parties (we hope).

THE ENTREPRENEURIAL SPIRIT

From everything previously mentioned, it is clear that anyone entering this wide-open field must have a sense of adventure, of walking off the beaten track, in short, of possessing that elusive spirit of the entrepreneur. The weak-kneed need not apply nor those who insist on painting by the numbers.

If you enjoy your fellow humans, relish a challenge, are making a decent living at whatever you are doing, and fancy yourself in a room full of conflicted people, knowing that you are the one who can help them all get along, you may have what it takes. You are setting up your own practice in a dynamic new field which most of your potential clients walking on the street outside your office know nothing about. You are a pioneer breaking new ground. How many of your friends and colleagues can claim the same?

A STRONG CODE OF ETHICS: Any healthy mediation practice is grounded in a strong sense of ethics. You have a duty to adhere to a professional code. Broad categories to be considered include:
- The Responsibility of the Mediator to the Parties.
- The Responsibility of the Mediator to the Mediation Process.
- The Responsibility of the Mediator to Other Mediators.
- The Responsibility of the Mediator to His or Her Agency and Profession.
- The Responsibility of the Mediator to the Public and Other Unrepresented Parties.

A complete model code is included in Appendix B of this book. *Please study it carefully.*

FIFTEEN

Launching Your Ship

FINDING A LOCATION

I encourage the beginning mediator to share office space with a psychotherapist, an attorney, a CPA, or the like, or to find an executive office suite setup. At the beginning, you will want to keep your overhead as low as possible. You need a high-quality location that presents a professional image, that is easy to find, and is readily accessible to the population you will serve.

SPACE REQUIREMENTS AND OFFICE EQUIPMENT

You need a mediation room that is at least 15 by 15 square feet. It must be large enough to have a round table and four chairs plus an area for filing cabinets, computer and printer, telephone, fax machine, copier and an easel with a newsprint flip chart. You will also need a coffee maker, an electric boiler for making tea water, a water pitcher and glasses. And it is really nice to add a touch of class by setting the table with a white tablecloth and flowers.

You also need a waiting area outside the meeting room where your clients can move to during one-on-one coaching sessions as well as wait for their mediation session to begin. This is why I

Set Up Practice

recommend finding an executive suite or sharing office space with someone else.

MARKETING AND ADVERTISING

First, determine your target market. Then reach that market by advertising in periodicals that your market will read. For example, if you are pursuing the divorce market, focus on divorcing couples and consider taking out an ad in the classified section of your local daily newspaper. If your target is the business community, run advertisements in local business journals and business weekly magazines. If you plan to address the church market, you need to run ads in denominational newsletters or national periodicals read by church leaders.

Public speaking is an excellent way to become known. Identify the groups which your potential clients belong to. Rotary Clubs, PTA's, Bar Association Meetings, professional gatherings of CPA's, in-service training programs for social workers and ministerial associations will do for starters.

How do you reach these groups? Pick up the phone and call them. Tell them that you are a mediator, that you provide a mediation service in town, and that you would like to offer a free 20-minute presentation on mediation at their next luncheon. Believe me, they will respond.

Another way to reach your market is to write articles about mediation for your local newspaper. Read the newspaper carefully, then write three sample columns. If you do not know how to write for public media, learn fast. Follow the style and length of the other columns in the newspaper on your first draft, then personalize it on your final draft. Use a question/answer format or pick a subject for each column. Bring in human interest stories to make your point. Think of a catchy standing headline so readers will recognize your column each time.

Set up an appointment with the managing editor. Bring along your credentials and sample columns. The editor will appreciate your novel idea as well as tangible proof that you can write when he or she sees your three columns ready for publication.

Issue news releases typed on your company letterhead with your name and phone number at the top. Nothing gripes busy editors more than seeing a strangely-spelled name or unclear sentence on a news release with no phone number to call and verify.

If anything significant happens in your business, whether you open your new practice, receive an award or bring a colleague into your mediation firm, send releases to your local newspapers, magazines, radio and TV stations. Send to a specific editor in a specific department. NEVER send a news release to the women's editor, the business editor and the real estate editor at the same time. Your local newspaper will have egg on its face when all three of the same releases run the same day. You will be on their black list forever. Check out a library book on public relations, preferably one written within the past five years.

Offer your services to a call-in radio talk show. This is a dynamic way to bring your name before the public and spread the word about mediation. I have had some real fun with this one!

YOUR BROCHURE, BUSINESS CARDS AND STATIONERY

It is worth the money to hire a professional firm to put together your brochure, blending graphics and copy to communicate your message. Your brochure must produce a high-quality image worthy of your services. Use the same graphics on your business cards and business letterhead. Look in the Yellow Pages under "Graphic Designers" or "Advertising Agencies," ask for samples and a rate sheet, and select the firm whose brochures and business cards look the best. Choose people who will listen to your ideas and collaborate with you. Remember to keep careful records of all business expenses for your taxes.

YOUR TELEPHONE SYSTEM

Can't afford a receptionist or secretary at first? That's fine. You need a sophisticated voice mail system where people can call in 24 hours a day to receive concrete, detailed information on the services you provide and, if desired, leave a message so you or a colleague can return their calls. Do not even think of cutting costs by subscribing to an answering service or installing an inexpensive answering machine.

Remember how frustrated you felt when the answering service barely had five seconds to take down your message? These workers make about $5 an hour and have 30 switchboard lines to answer. Remember when you were cut off while trying to record a message on someone's answering machine...or it beeped eight times, you started talking, then felt like a fool when it beeped again? Do you want people to feel the same red hot rage when they try to reach you?

Study voice mail systems carefully before you buy. Find one that is listener-friendly. Imagine you are your prospective client at the other end. Choose a system that supplies easy, clear instructions, which allows the caller to leave a detailed message without being cut off. Let the prospective client know in your pre-recorded message that he can speak as long as he desires. *Do unto others as you would have them do unto you.*

In our culture you must respond to your callers within one working day or less. When you are out of the office or out of town, check in with your voice mail system and return messages promptly. Just as a rude receptionist in a large corporation can smear the most expensive advertising campaigns, your telephone etiquette is synonymous with your direct, face-to-face advertising outreach program. Fail in this and your business will suffer.

FEE STRUCTURE

A typical fee structure ranges from $80 to $180 per hour for the mediator's time. Domestic cases usually fall in the lower end of the scale; business and commercial cases tend to be higher. For organizational mediation — corporations, municipalities, churches, etc. — the fees range from $800 to $1200 per day. You will want to have a simple rate sheet or include these fees in your brochure. Specify the fee in your written contracts with your clients.

It is equally important to get a non-refundable deposit up front that covers a third of your total anticipated fees. The parties in the dispute equally share the fees. Have the parties pay for each session at the beginning of each session. For a smooth payment of fees, explain this procedure to all key persons when scheduling the first session.

IN ESSENCE...

- Keep your present job.

- Attend a mediation training session.

- Volunteer for a public mediation center, enroll in a private mediation firm's internship program, or contract for long-distance consultation.

- You won't earn a million dollars as a mediator but intrinsic rewards will come your way.

- Only entrepreneurs need apply.

- Share office space or use an executive suite.

- Do not cut corners on office equipment.

- Determine your market. Advertise through the media or via public speaking, columns in your local newspaper, news releases and call-in radio talk shows.

- Do not cut corners on your brochure, business cards, letterhead or voice mail system.

- Return phone calls promptly.

- Obtain a non-refundable deposit up front and the day's fees before each session.

PART FIVE

The Question & Answer Forum

The Question and Answer Forum

The following questions are those most frequently asked by clients and graduate students:

• *Is mediation the practice of law or of psychotherapy?*

It is neither. Mediation is the distinct practice of dispute resolution which may involve an understanding of law and some elements and skills drawn from psychotherapy. But it is its own unique profession. Often mediation creates a "psychotherapeutic effect" in which healing takes place, but this is a by-product and not the central purpose of mediation. Mediation involves a knowledge of law, but the mediator must never give legal advice.

• *Is mediation appropriate in domestic violence situations or when a party is under the influence of drugs?*

The debate continues to rage over this issue. Some mediators will not handle domestic violence situations under any circumstance. Many others choose to mediate these same cases. This is an ethical decision that you as a mediator will have to make. In my practice, I have chosen to mediate cases in which domestic violence has been perpetrated as long as the physical safety of all parties involved is insured during the mediation. I will never refuse to mediate disputes where there is verbal abuse. I will not mediate a case in which either party is intoxicated or under the influence of drugs.

• *Are some people so disagreeable that mediation will not work?*

In Susan Heitler's book, *From Conflict to Resolution (p.63)*, the author points out four symptoms to look for in dysfunctional people. I have discovered that these apply consistently to clients who are not appropriate for mediation:

1) When individuals cause undue emotional pain to others.

2) When they continue to yield no solutions to the problems, electing to remain mired in the muck of the dispute and enjoy the in-fighting for as long as possible.

3) When they continually satisfy their own needs at the expense of all the needs of the other people.

4) When they manifest other symptoms such as depression, anxiety and addictions.

Unless the mediator can find a way to get through to folks who manifest this dysfunctional pattern, mediation may be futile. These clients often sabotage the process. Some people keep conflict alive to maintain an unhealthy interrelatedness, to reinforce a self image as a tiger, or to stay in a martyr's position.

• *Is professional liability insurance available for mediators?*

Yes. Contact one of the professional organizations listed in Appendix D of this book. Specialized insurance is geared to the specific needs of mediators and arbitrators. I encourage mediators to take out liability insurance, although there have been only a handful of cases in the United States where mediator malpractice has been claimed. The cost is reasonable — generally $250-$350 per year. If you are a mediator from another profession, check with your liability insurance company to see if it provides a rider for mediation.

• *I have heard about co-mediation. What are the advantages and disadvantages?*

Co-mediation is when you and another mediator work together as a duo to help the disputants settle their conflict. In our firm we highly value co-mediation and tend to use it as a norm, for two reasons. First, it gives you a partner with whom you can bounce off ideas, and with whom you share your frustrations and the pressures of negotiation. With a co-mediator, you design strategies that work and obtain a second perspective. Moreover, the sessions run much smoother.

The disadvantages: If you work with someone you do not know very well or with whom you enter power plays, the mediation may be a disaster. You must be in sync with each other; there must be give and take between the two of you.

• *What is Med/Arb?*

Med/Arb is a hybrid dispute resolution process that begins with mediation and ends with arbitration. In Med/Arb, the parties mediate as many of the issues as they can. If they reach a roadblock in the resolution of their issues, the neutral third party takes off his/her mediator hat and puts on an arbitrator hat. After listening to all sides of the case and receiving testimony, the dispute resolver renders a binding decision. This is called Med/Arb (same). In Med/Arb (different), the case is turned over to a new and different third party to arbitrate the case after the mediation phase. Med/Arb is receiving high marks in client satisfaction. It is the dispute resolution mechanism that I prefer. You can help people facilitate a settlement of their issues. Then, if they cannot go any further, these same disputants turn over the case to you for settlement so there is a full and final resolution brought to the dispute.

• *What professional mediation organizations do you recommend that I join?*

Academy of Family Mediators, American Association of Family Counselors and Mediators, Association of Family and Conciliation Courts, and Society of Professionals in Dispute Resolution. Complete addresses and phone numbers are listed in Appendix D of this book.

These organizations will offer you:
- Excellent journals.
- Regular newsletters.
- Professional relationships.
- Networking opportunities.
- Conferences for education and renewal.

• *As a beginning mediator, should I specialize in one type of mediation?*

No, I encourage you first to become a *general practitioner*. Note the two types of mediation. The first is *process-focused mediation*, where you become a dispute resolution specialist. You understand the dynamics and the process and the rhythm and the movement of helping bring people to settlement. The second is *substance-focused mediation*. Here, you the mediator are a substantive expert on the topic of the dispute; namely, family law, environmental law, medical issues, etc.

I recommend that you become a process-focused mediator, that you truly learn the process of dispute resolution. You will find that you can apply this new paradigm to myriad dispute situations. Later, you can move to a specialized area of interest, if desired.

• *What are the main reasons your clients have given as to why they like mediation?*

A few reasons are cited again and again. Number one, mediation is less expensive — approximately a third the cost of fighting in court. Several years ago I worked with a wealthy divorcing couple. It was a complex mediation: lots of property and lots of children. The couple spent a total of $3,000 on the mediation. Both of their high-powered divorce attorneys were in awe of how little they spent, and said that, had they litigated their divorce, each would have paid between $38,000 and $42,000.

Second, clients tell me that mediation has helped them retain power over their own lives. Rather than have a settlement imposed on them, they were able to create their own solutions.

Third, they were able to survive their disputes without destroying one another, and then get on with their lives. Although the process was rough, painful at times, often some mending of relationships and psychological healing was achieved.

Fourth, they tell me that their agreements were crafted and customized to their unique situation, never a boilerplate solution.

• *What is "success" in mediation?*

For me, success generally means that the clients resolve all of their issues, that they reach closure. In some cases, the ones where you cannot reach a 100 percent settlement, i.e., a full and final agreement, you still may have been successful in that you have opened up the lines of communication, you have allowed people to vent, and you have given them for the first time a forum that is safe to share their perspectives. Thus, success defined as 100 percent settlement may not always be the bottom line. It may embrace these secondary gains.

I once supervised an intern who mediated a highly contentious divorce case in the courthouse. After hours of sweaty work, the couple resolved all the issues. Then the surprise came. Rather than going directly into court as planned to file their final papers, they told the mediator how she had helped them communicate better for the first time in twenty years, thanked her, held hands and left the courthouse. The intern stood on the steps with her mouth wide open! Success varies from case to case.

• *Have you ever terminated a mediation by "firing the client?"*

Yes, on rare occasions. I have needed to do that when there has been relentless and ongoing physical abuse or when one of the parties decided that the dispute had best be resolved in court to set a legal precedent and to continue in mediation would abrogate his or her rights.

• *How do you assess the future of mediation as a profession?*

Mediation has been called the boom industry of the 21st Century. This era is breaking in upon us now. A tremendous market is out there. The problem is that at this point in history, millions of people do not even know that mediation exists. You have an obligation to educate the world about this new and wonderful way of resolving disputes. The future of mediation? It's limitless.

• *Are attorneys and judges supportive of mediation?*

Attorney bashing has become great sport in this country. But the vast majority of lawyers with whom I have worked are highly supportive of mediation as an alternative to litigation. There is a movement afoot to require lawyers to inform their clients of ADR options.

The Colorado Supreme Court, responding to a proposal from the Colorado State Bar Association, recently adopted an amendment to its ethics rules encouraging lawyers to inform their clients of ADR options.

Judges have been most supportive of mediation. Many disputes require traditional litigation with a judge or a jury. Mediation eases the grueling courtroom schedule, freeing the court calendar for these cases.

• *How long does a typical mediation take from start to finish?*

In studying my records, I found the average time to be five to seven sessions of 1.5 to 2.0 hours each. Some are much shorter and others much longer.

• *In everything I read regarding mediation, I find that the mediator must be "neutral." Is there really such a thing as neutrality?*

I do not believe that there is such a thing as absolute neutrality. Every third party, indeed every human being, brings his or her own history, background, values and world view to the mediation table. The concepts of neutrality and impartiality have become sacred cows in many mediation circles. However, let us remember what Abbie Hoffman said, "Sacred cows make the tastiest hamburger."

I think it important that the mediator favor neither side in the dispute and have no vested interest in the outcome. The mediator should stand "equidistant" from each party during the mediation.

It is imperative that each mediator be in touch with his or her own biases, values and limitations in order to serve as a third party. I recommend that every prospective mediator go to the Tolerance Museum in Los Angeles. Before entering the main exhibit area, one must make a choice between two entrances — one marked "For Those With Prejudice;" the other named, "For Those Without Prejudice."

The latter is locked and cannot be used.

Remember, neutrality is like virginity. Once it is gone, it is gone forever.

• *Please explain the concept of confidentiality.*

Mediation thrives in an environment where honest dialogue flows. If a party is afraid that something revealed in mediation will later be used against him or her, then communication will be stifled or shut down. Confidentiality ensures that all communication will be kept as privileged information between the mediator and the client system. This atmosphere of openness is critical.

A disclaimer: In my practice, I do not guarantee absolute confidentiality. I reserve the right to break confidentiality in specific circumstances, as outlined in Part Three of this book. They are repeated here:

- All parties and the mediator consent in writing to disclose mediation communications.
- The communication reveals the intent to commit a felony, inflict bodily harm, or threaten the safety of a child under the age of 18.
- The communication is required by statute to be made public.
- Disclosure is necessary and relevant to an action alleging willful and wanton misconduct of the mediator or the Center for Solutions, Inc.

It is vital that you are up front with your clients about any exclusions which you may invoke. Equally important, you need to study any state laws which govern the issue of mediation confidentiality. More than 250 state and federal statutes and many decisions have to do with mediation confidentiality.

• *What are your cardinal rules for mediators?*
- Always remember that the dispute belongs to the disputants and not to you. It is their conflict, not yours.
- Be clear that the solution is theirs and not yours.
- Respect each and every disputant as a valuable human being.

- Apply the Golden Rule in the mediation room.
- Let go of the stress and conflicts you experience every night before going to bed.
- Do not take yourself too seriously!

• *Tell me about mandatory, court-ordered mediation.*

Many courts now require disputants to mediate prior to seeking a resolution through litigation. From my perspective, mandatory mediation is an oxymoron, for mediation is based on freedom, choice, empowerment, and self-determination of the outcome.

I have seen numerous court-ordered clients who enter the mediation room hostile because they feel manipulated; they do not want to be there. I always tell these clients: "You have been ordered to come to mediation. But no one can make you mediate. By coming here, you have fulfilled the order of the court. Now, is there anything I can do to help you folks work this out?" Words like this give people permission to terminate or to choose to buy into the process and give it a try. They usually choose the latter.

• *What is your dream for dispute resolution in the future?*

I envision a public dispute resolution center in each and every community. Disputants will schedule an intake interview with a dispute resolution specialist. The disputants, their attorneys and the specialist will assess the case and assign it to the appropriate ADR forum: self-negotiation, mediation, arbitration, Med/Arb or some other methodology. The disputing parties will then proceed to a specific room in the center where the case will be settled. Courts will then be freed up to do what courts do best, to deal with hardcore cases and issues of real justice. This bright new future awaits you!

EPILOGUE

The Hundredth Monkey

Several years ago I heard a story about the Hundredth Monkey. It impacted my life and I want to share it with you, in closing.

For three decades, a community of monkeys has lived on a chain of islands off the coast of Japan. On one island, some scientists often tossed sweet potatoes in the sand. That was in 1952. The monkeys enjoyed the sweet potatoes but not the dirt.

Several months went by. A baby monkey began washing the potatoes in the stream. Pleased with herself, she taught this new skill to her mother and to other little monkeys who in turn showed the new technique to their mothers. Soon all the young monkeys were washing their potatoes. But only the grown-ups who were taught by their children changed their behavior. The other adult monkeys ate unwashed sweet potatoes.

Five years passed. The scientists noted that, on one particular autumn day in 1958, a certain number of monkeys were washing their potatoes. Since we do not know that number, we shall call it X. Later that day, X plus one monkeys were washing potatoes. In that small, seemingly insignificant act of adding one monkey to the fold, a quantum act shook the psychic barrier of ignorance. *That evening, nearly every monkey in the tribe was washing potatoes. Even more astounding, monkey colonies on other islands and on the mainland suddenly and mysteriously began washing their sweet potatoes.*

No one knows exactly how many monkeys were washing sweet potatoes that day on the island. To make it elegant, let us say that it was 99. The added energy of the 100th monkey pushed something over the edge, creating a breakthrough in consciousness that transcended time and distance. Scientists state it in these terms: that when a certain critical number achieves an awareness, this awareness may be communicated from mind to mind.

The Hundredth Monkey Phenomenon has since become a password. It means that when a new idea is shared by a small group of people, it remains the property of these people. But somewhere along the line, when one more person embraces that idea, it is no longer the property of the few but of the world.

I have dedicated a part of my life to teaching people one by one about the benefits of mediation. Before I die, I hope to reach the Hundredth Monkey. For then the whole world will be transformed.

As Shepherd Mead said: "If we want to make something really superb on this planet, there is nothing whatever that can stop us."

So get going NOW!

APPENDICES

APPENDIX A

Sample Mediation Agreement

DISTRICT COURT, COUNTY OF DENVER, COLORADO
Case No.: 91DR348
Div/CtRm: #4

Memorandum of Agreement (A Mediated Settlement)

In re the Marriage of:
Millard J. Simpson, Petitioner and
Wilma A. Simpson, Co-Petitioner

This is an Agreement made and entered into by and between the persons named in the caption above.

Both Parties agree that the marriage is irretrievably broken, meaning that there are differences in the marriage which cannot be worked out or reconciled.

Relevant statistical information for the purpose of this proceeding is:

The Petitioner: Millard J. Simpson
>   Current Address: 131 First St. Ct., Heightsville, CO, 80241
>   Residency in Colorado: 18 years
>   Age of Petitioner: 43
>   The Petitioner is not a member of the armed services stationed in Colorado.

The Co-Petitioner: Wilma A. Simpson
>   Current Address: 112 Humboldt St., Heightsville, CO 80233
>   Residency in Colorado: 18 years
>   Age of Petitioner: 45
>   The Co-Petitioner is not a member of the armed services stationed in Colorado.

Marital and Separation Data:
>   Date of Marriage: 9/10/68
>   Place of Marriage: Torrance, Ohio
>   Length of Marriage: 22.5 years
>   Date of Separation: 3/2/91
>   The Wife is not pregnant

Name, address, birth date and age of children born or adopted during this marriage:

Nezzie Lynn Simpson, 112 Humboldt St., Heightsville, CO. 80233 (with mother) and 131 First St. Ct., Heightsville, CO. 80241 (with father), age 9 (DOB: 9/8/81)

The following terms of this Agreement were developed through Mediation at the Center for Solutions. This document represents a fair and equitable settlement of all issues between the Parties, as attested to by the signatures below. The terms agreed to herein are those negotiated between the Parties. Each party to this Memorandum of Agreement has been advised by the mediator that it is important that each of them take this document to a lawyer for legal advice regarding the contents of said document.

IT IS UNDERSTOOD AND AGREED BY BOTH PARTIES AS FOL-
LOWS:

I. PARTIES

It is agreed that after signing this Agreement, the Parties shall live separately and apart from one another, each to be free from the marital control
and authority of the other Party. Neither Party shall make debts, charges,
or liabilities whatsoever for which the other Party shall or may become
liable.

II. PARENTING PLAN

1. The Parties agree that it is in the best interest of the child that a friendly
and harmonious relationship exist between the Parties hereto with regard to the child, and therefore the Parties do hereby stipulate and agree
that neither shall demean or belittle the other before the minor child
and further that neither Party shall attempt to influence the minor child
unfavorably toward the other Party. The Parties recognize that the child
is happiest when she sees each of her parents without dissension appear-
ing.

a.The Parties acknowledge that both are dedicated parents who, although divorcing, want their daughter, Nezzie Lynn, to have a meaningful
and positive relationship with each parent. The Parties share a common
concern for their daughter.

b.Any specific time-sharing schedule has to first conform to Nezzie's
needs as much as possible, understanding that these needs will change
over time.

c.Currently, the Parties believe that it is important for their daughter to share time with each of them equally.

d.These parents acknowledge and affirm that it is important for them
to maintain communication and a cooperative relationship regarding
the parenting of Nezzie.

2.Custody: The Parties agree to joint legal custody and to mutually make
all major decisions regarding the health, education, child care and general welfare of their minor child.

a.Regarding religious activities, each parent will make said decisions
when Nezzie is in their respective homes.

b.Each parent will make his and her best effort to share information
with the other parent regarding Nezzie's school, friendships and activities.

c.Each Party hereby affirms their trust in the other's parenting judgement, and declares that the provisions about and for making joint major decisions impacting Nezzie's life are not intended to restrain the other parent from making day-to-day decisions while she is in each parent's care and physical custody.

3.Legal Residence: The Parties have agreed upon and established a shared physical custody arrangement. However, the legal address of the minor child shall be listed as her mother's residence.

4.Physical Custody and Time-Sharing:

a.The Parties agree that it is in their child's best interest for them to maintain shared physical custody.

b.Nezzie will spend equal amounts of time in each parent's home, rotating her residence on a weekly basis. The exchange time shall be 6:00 P.M. each Sunday.

c.Transportation arrangements will be made by the parent with whom Nezzie is staying.

d.Holidays will be shared equally, as mutually agreed upon and set by both Parties. A specific holiday schedule has been developed for 1994 and 1995.

e.Each parent may take vacations with Nezzie not to exceed two weeks each calendar year. A minimum of four weeks' notice will be given to the other parent. When the vacation ends, the regular established parenting schedule will resume.

f.Vacations or business trips without Nezzie:

1)If possible, a minimum of two weeks' notice will be provided to the other parent.

2)It is the responsibility of the parent who will be gone to arrange for Nezzie's care during the time she is scheduled to be with the absent parent.

3)When the parent returns, the regular established parenting schedule will resume.

g.Each Party will insure that Nezzie continues to have a positive relationship with members of each of their extended families.

h.Schedule Changes and Flexibility: The Parties agree to notify the other Party of any changes to the schedule as soon as possible in the event a change is needed. The schedule can be changed by prior notice and mutual consent.

5.Emergency Medical Care and Notification: If an emergency occurs, the parent responsible at the time (per the parenting schedule) will make every reasonable effort to contact the other parent. However, if the other parent is not available, the responsible parent will take appropriate action immediately (such as seeking medical treatment).

6. Moving:

a.In order to facilitate each parent's visitation with the child, the time-sharing plan as written in this section will remain in effect as long as the Parties reside within the Denver/Heightsville area.

b.In the event that either Party anticipates a move more than twenty-five (25) miles outside of this specified geographical area, the Parties will renegotiate the current time-sharing arrangement and develop a mutually agreeable plan.

III. CHILD SUPPORT & OTHER FINANCIAL SUPPORT

1.Child Support: It is further agreed that Millard shall pay child support directly to Wilma by personal check in the amount of $137.00 per month, due and payable on the first day of each month. Child Support payments are to begin October 1, 1994, and shall continue until the child reaches the age of emancipation or 19, whichever occurs first.

The Parties understand that the provisions of a child support order may be modified only if there is a substantial and continuing change of circumstances (such as income, number of overnights spent in each home, etc.). If application of the Guideline would result in a new order that is less than ten percent different, then the circumstances are considered not to be a substantial and continuing change.

The Parties agree to review the Child Support annually in August of each year. In the event of remarriage by either Party, they agree to base child support on each parent's individual income and not the joint income with the new spouse(s).

2.Child Rearing Expenses: In that the Parties have shared physical custody of the minor child, they agree to share in child rearing expense and to pay for said expenses when the child resides with them. These expenses include, but are not limited to, clothing, babysitting, work-related child care costs (which are shared equally) and other expenses as mutually agreed upon.

3.Health Care and Costs: Health insurance on the minor child shall be maintained by Millard, as long as it is available through his employment.

a.Nonreimbursable medical expenses (including dental and orthodontic) will be paid by each Party proportionate to their incomes on a percentage basis.

b.If any change in the above arrangements occurs (such as loss of coverage, change in benefits, etc.), the Parties agree to notify the other parent as soon as possible.

4.Higher Education: The Parties agree in principle that their daughter Nezzie should have the opportunity to attend college. They agree to jointly assist in arranging for college and will provide some financial support. They further agree that Nezzie will be expected to pay some portion of her college fees. The Parties will review this issue in Nezzie's second year of high school and at that time will negotiate a more defined plan of action.

5.Life Insurance:

a.Wilma does not currently carry life insurance. The issue will be reviewed by no later than June, 1994.

b.Millard agrees to maintain life insurance naming himself as the insured with a minimum value of $100,000. and naming Nezzie as the beneficiary.

IV. SPOUSAL MAINTENANCE (ALIMONY)

It is further agreed that both Parties do not want Maintenance and give up any right to spousal maintenance, whether temporary or permanent. Both Parties know that they may never, in the future, ask for Maintenance from the other Party.

V. DISPOSITION OF ASSETS AND LIABILITIES

ASSETS

1.Each Party affirms that she and/or he has fully disclosed all property of value owned by him or her or by the marriage including (but not limited to) all vested rights in pensions, annuity, disability, life insurance, and/or military benefit plans or awards.

The Parties acknowledge that any asset acquired before this marriage, or by gift or by inheritance, together with his or her own clothes, papers, and other personal effects will remain the sole and separate property of the person acquiring said asset. All other assets are joint and are to be divided as agreed to in this document.

The Parties understand that joint assets are mutually owned by them, no matter how titled or possessed. The Parties agree to execute all necessary legal documents to transfer property from joint ownership to individual ownership as agreed to in this Agreement no later than 30 days following the dissolution, unless otherwise agreed upon and noted below. Any property not otherwise specified in this Agreement shall remain with the spouse now having possession.

2.Real Estate: The Parties agree that Millard will have sole occupancy and ownership of the former marital home located at 131 First St. Court, Heightsville, CO. The estimated property value is $70,000. with a loan balance of approximately $65,000. The Parties determined that the equity in the home is approximately $5,000; and said equity will be Millard's sole and separate property. Wilma has assigned all of her interest in this property over to Millard by a Quit Claim Deed. Millard is solely responsible for the loan and all house-related expenses; and Millard does indemnify and hold Wilma harmless for all such encumbrances, payments, and expenses.

The Parties agree that Wilma will have sole occupancy and ownership of the home located at 112 Humboldt Street, Heightsville, CO. The Parties acknowledge that, as a part of the equitable settlement and to equalize real estate assets between them, Millard provided the down payment for Wilma to purchase this home. The property is valued at approximately $65,000. The Parties agree that the current equity in this property is approximately $5200 and that said equity is the sole and separate property of Wilma. Wilma is solely responsible for the loan and all house-related expenses; and Wilma does indemnify and hold Millard harmless for all such encumbrances, payments, and expenses.

3.Businesses: Each Party owns his own business. The Parties agree that neither person shall have any claim to any value of the other person's business assets both now and in the future.

4.Wilma's Trust Fund: Gladys Bird, grandmother of Wilma, has established a Trust naming Wilma as beneficiary and trustee. The Parties agree that Millard has no claim to this Trust both now and in the future.

5.Household Goods: All have been divided fairly and moved to each Party's respective home.

6.Motor Vehicles:

a.Millard shall have as his sole and separate property the following described automobiles:

1)The Mitsubishi Montero, titled in Millard's name. The value is approximately $16,000 with loan balance of approximately $16,000. Millard is solely responsible for making payments to First Interstate Bank of Denver.

2)Mazda Truck, titled in Millard's name. The value is approximately $2000. with no encumbrance.

b.Wilma shall have as her sole and separate property the following described automobile: 1991 Honda CRX, titled in Wilma's name. The value is approximately $14,730. with loan balance of approximately $10,575. Wilma is solely responsible for making payments to Bank of Denver.

7.Bank Accounts: Bank accounts have been separated. Each Party will keep each account listed solely in his or her name.

DEBTS AND OBLIGATIONS

1.Debt Settlement (Husband): It is further agreed that the following debts, including any other obligations and costs arising out of this action, will be paid as follows by the Husband:

- American Express, held in Millard's name.
- VISA Debit Card, held in Millard's name.
- Mastercard Debit, held in Millard's name.
- Security Pacific, held in Millard's name.
- Penny's, held in Millard's name.
- Mervyn's, held in Millard's name.
- May D and F, held in Millard's name.
- First Mortgage.
- First Interstate Auto Loan.

2.Debt Settlement (Wife): It is further agreed that the following debts, including any other obligations and costs arising out of this action, will be paid as follows by the Wife:

- McDuff, held in Wilma's name.
- Mervyn's, held in Wilma's name.
- American Express Platinum, held in Wilma's name.
- American Express Corporate, held in Wilma's name.
- CitiBank Mastercard, held in Wilma's name.
- Chase Manhattan VISA, held in Wilma's name.
- Penny's, held in Wilma's name.

- Holy Roads Mortgage.
- Central Bank Auto Loan.

Hold Harmless Clause: It is the intention of the Parties to hold the other Party harmless from all debts assigned to him or her individually as noted above. If the Party who agrees to pay a debt does not complete payment, that Party must reimburse the other Party for any payments, costs, or legal fees incurred by the other Party in paying or defending against the debt.

VI. JURISDICTION

The Parties agree that this District Court shall have continued jurisdiction over the child of this marriage and the Parties regarding custody, visitation, and child support. The Parties agree that the laws of the State of Colorado shall be the law applied to the Parties, this Agreement, and this dissolution of marriage action. All modifications of this agreement shall be in writing and filed with the court.

VII. DISPUTE RESOLUTION

In the event that any further dispute arises between the Parties regarding the provisions of this Agreement, or otherwise related to their dissolution of marriage or their ongoing shared parenting responsibilities, which they are unable to resolve themselves, they agree to return to mediation to attempt to resolve the matter before seeking a resolution in court.

VIII. FAIRNESS

Each Party, by signing this Agreement, certifies that she and/or he has read and understood the Agreement, and that the contents are reasonable to each other, and state what each Party believes she and/or he is entitled to under the Uniform Dissolution of Marriage Act of Colorado.

The Parties understand that important legal rights and responsibilities are addressed in this Agreement. By their signatures, they acknowledge that they are responsible for all terms listed herein; and that the Center for Solutions has assisted them in mediating the terms of this agreement and providing typing services of the necessary forms based on information provided by the Parties. In no way has the Center provided legal advice.

Each Party has had such legal advice from an attorney in reaching this Agreement as she and/or he desires and/or has decided to file this action Pro Se (Do-It-Yourself); and enters into this Agreement freely and voluntarily.

IX. INCORPORATION OF THIS AGREEMENT
INTO THE FINAL DECREE

What is written in this Agreement shall be added to the Final Decree by this District Court, and when this Agreement is added to the final Decree, shall have full force and effect of an Order by this Court, and shall be enforceable. Any costs and fees incurred in enforcing this Agreement shall be paid by the Party found by the Court to be in non-compliance with the Agreement.

_____   _____
Millard J. Simpson   Date

_____   _____
Wilma A. Simpson   Date

APPENDIX B

COLORADO COUNCIL OF MEDIATION ORGANIZATIONS
Code of Professional Conduct (1982)

PREAMBLE

Mediation is an approach to conflict resolution in which an impartial third party intervenes in a dispute, with the consent of the parties, to aid and assist them in reaching a mutually satisfactory settlement to issues in dispute.

Mediation is a profession with ethical responsibilities and duties. Those who engage in the practice of mediation must be dedicated to the principle that all disputants have a right to negotiate and to attempt to determine the outcomes of their own conflicts. Mediators must be aware that their duties and obligations relate to the parties who engage their services, to the mediation process, to other mediators, to the agencies that administer the practice of mediation, and to the general public.

Mediators are often professionals (attorneys, therapists and social workers) who have obligations under other codes of ethics. This code is not to be construed as a competitive code of behavior but as an additional guideline for professionals performing mediation. When mediating, professionals will be bound by the ethical guidelines of this code.

This code is not designed to override or supersede any laws or government regulations that prescribe responsibilities of mediators and others in the helping professions. It is a personal code of conduct for the individual mediator and is intended to establish principles applicable to all professional mediators employed by private, city, state, or federal agencies.

1. Responsibility of the Mediator to the Parties

The primary responsibility for the resolution of a dispute rests on the parties themselves. The mediator should recognize at all times that the agreements reached in negotiations are voluntarily made by the parties. It is the mediator's responsibility to assist the disputants in reaching a settlement. At no time should a mediator coerce a party into agreement. The mediator should not attempt to make a substantive decision for the parties. Parties may, however, agree to solicit a recommendation for settlement from the mediator.

It is desirable that agreement be reached by negotiations without a mediator's assistance. Intervention by a mediator can be initiated by the parties themselves or by a mediator. The decision to accept mediation rests with the parties, except when mediation is mandated by legislation, court order, or contract.

Mediators will inform all parties of the cost of mediation services before intervention. Parties should be able to estimate the cost of the service in relation to that of other dispute resolution procedures.

Ideally, when costs are involved, the mediator should attempt to have parties agree to bear the costs of mediation equitably. When this is not possible, all parties should reach agreement as to payment.

2. Responsibility of the Mediator to the Mediation Process

Negotiation is an established procedure in our society as a means of resolving disputes. The process of mediation involves a third-party intervention into negotiations to assist in the development of alternative solutions that parties will voluntarily accept as a basis for settlement. Pressures that jeopardize voluntary action and agreement by the parties should not be a part of mediation.

The Mediation Process

Mediation is a participatory process. A mediator is obliged to educate the parties and to involve them in the mediation process. A mediator should consider that such education and involvement are important not only to resolve a current dispute but also to prepare the parties to handle future conflicts in a more creative and productive manner.

Appropriateness of Mediation

Mediation is not a panacea for all types of conflicts. Mediators should be aware of all procedures for dispute resolution and the conditions under which each is most effective. Mediators are obliged to educate participants as to their procedural options and to help them choose wisely the most appropriate procedures. The procedures should clearly match the type of outcome that is desired by the parties.

Mediator's Role

The mediator must not limit his or her role to keeping the peace or regulating conflict at the bargaining table. The mediator's role should be that of an active resource person whom the parties may draw on and, when appropriate, the mediator should be prepared to provide both procedural and substantive suggestions and alternatives that will assist the parties in successful negotiations.

Since the status, experience, and ability of the mediator lend weight to his or her suggestions and recommendations, the mediator should evaluate carefully the effect of interventions or proposals and accept full responsibility for their honesty and merit.

Since mediation is a voluntary process, the acceptability of the mediator to the parties as a person of integrity, objectivity, and fairness is absolutely essential for the effective performance of mediation procedures. The manner in which the mediator carries out professional duties and responsibilities will be a measure of his or her usefulness as a mediator. The quality of character as well as intellectual, emotional, social, and technical attributes will reveal themselves in the conduct of the mediator and in his or her oral and written communications with the parties, other mediators, and the public.

Publicity and Advertising

A mediator should not make any false, misleading, or unfair statement or claim as to the mediation process, its costs and benefits, or his or her role, skills, or qualifications.

Neutrality

A mediator should determine and reveal all monetary, psychological, emotional, associational, or authoritative affiliations that he or she has with any of the parties to a dispute that might cause a conflict of interest or affect the perceived or actual neutrality of the professional in the performance of duties. If the mediator or any one of the major parties feel that the mediator's background will have or has had a potential to bias his or her performance, the mediator should disqualify himself or herself from performing the mediation service.

Impartiality

The mediator is obligated during the performance of professional services to maintain a posture of impartiality toward all involved parties. Impartiality is freedom from bias or favoritism either in word or action. Impartiality implies a commitment to aid all parties, as opposed to a single party, in reaching a mutually satisfactory agreement. Impartiality means that a mediator will not play an adversarial role in the process of dispute resolution.

Confidentiality

Information received by a mediator in confidence, private session, caucus, or joint session with the disputants is confidential and should not be revealed to parties outside the negotiations. Information received in caucus is not to be revealed in joint session without receiving prior permission from the party or person from whom the information was received.

The following exceptions shall be applied to the confidentiality rule: In the event of child abuse by one or more disputants or in a case in which a mediator discovers that a probable crime will be committed that may result in serious psychological or physical harm to another person, the mediator is obligated to report these actions to the appropriate agencies.

Use of Information

Because information revealed in mediation is confidential and the success of the process may depend on this confidentiality, mediators should inform and gain consent from participants that information divulged in the process of mediation will not be used by the parties in any further adversarial proceedings.

The mediator is also obligated to resist disclosure of confidential information in an adversarial process. He or she will refuse to testify voluntarily in any subsequent court proceedings and shall resist to the best of his or her ability the subpoena of either his or her notes or person. This provision may be waived by the consent of all parties involved.

Empowerment

In the event that a party needs either additional information or assistance in order for the negotiations to proceed in a fair and orderly manner or for an agreement to be reached that is fair, equitable, and has the capacity to hold over time, the mediator is obligated to refer the party to resources — either data or persons — who may facilitate the process.

Psychological Well-Being

If a mediator discovers before or during mediation that a party needs psychological help, the mediator shall make appropriate referrals. Mediators recognize that mediation is not an appropriate substitute for therapy and shall refer parties to the appropriate procedure. Mediation shall not be conducted with parties who are either intoxicated or who have major psychological disorders that seriously impair their judgment.

The Law

Mediators are not lawyers. At no time shall a mediator offer legal advice to parties in dispute. Mediators shall refer parties to appropriate attorneys for legal advice. This same code of conduct applies to mediators who are themselves trained in the law. The role of an impartial mediator should not be confused with that of an attorney who is an advocate for a client.

The Settlement

The goal of negotiation and mediation is a settlement that is seen as fair and equitable by all parties. The mediator's responsibility to the parties is to help them reach this kind of settlement.

Whenever possible, a mediator should develop a written statement that documents the agreements reached in mediation.

A mediator's satisfaction with the agreement is secondary to that of the parties.

In the event that an agreement is reached that a mediator feels (1) is illegal, (2) is grossly inequitable to one or more parties, (3) is the result of false information, (4) is the result of bargaining in bad faith, (5) is impossible to enforce, or (6) may not hold over time, the mediator may pursue any or all of the following alternatives:

1. Inform the parties of the difficulties that the mediator sees in the agreement.
2. Inform the parties of the difficulties and make suggestions that would remedy the problems.
3. Withdraw as mediator without disclosing to either party the particular reasons for the withdrawal.

4. Withdraw as mediator but disclose in writing to both parties the reasons for such action.

5. Withdraw as mediator and reveal publicly the general reason for taking such action (Bargaining in bad faith, unreasonable settlement, illegality, and so forth).

Termination of Mediation

In the event that the parties cannot reach an agreement even with the assistance of a mediator, it is the responsibility of the mediator to make the parties aware of the deadlock and suggest that negotiations be terminated. A mediator is obligated to inform the parties when a final impasse has occurred and to refer them to other means of dispute resolution. A mediator should not prolong unproductive discussions that result in increased time and emotional and monetary costs for the parties.

3. The Responsibility of the Mediator to Other Mediators

A mediator should not enter any dispute that is being mediated by another mediator or mediators without first conferring with the person or persons conducting such mediations. The mediator should not intercede in a dispute merely because another mediator may also be participating. Conversely, it should not be assumed that the lack of mediation participation by one mediator indicates a need for participation by another mediator.

In those situations in which more than one mediator are participating in a particular case, each mediator has a responsibility to keep the others informed of developments essential to a cooperative effort and should extend every possible courtesy to co-mediators.

During mediation, the mediator should carefully avoid any appearance of disagreement with or criticism of co-mediators. Discussions as to what positions and actions mediators should take in particular cases should not violate principles of confidentiality.

4. The Responsibility of the Mediator to His or Her Agency and Profession

Mediators frequently work for agencies that are responsible for providing mediation assistance to parties in dispute. The mediator must recognize that as an employee of such agencies, the mediator is their representative, and that he or she will not be judged solely on an individual basis but also as a representative of an organization. Any improper conduct or professional shortcoming, therefore, reflects not only on the individual mediator but also on the employer, and in so doing, it jeopardizes the effectiveness of the agency, other agencies, and the acceptability of the mediation process itself.

The mediator should not use his or her position for personal gain or advantage or engage in any employment, activity, or enterprise that will conflict with his or her work as a mediator.

Mediators should not accept any money or item of value for the performance or services other than a regular salary or mutually established fee, or incur obligations to any party that might interfere with the impartial performance of his or her duties.

Training and Education

Mediators learn their trade through a variety of avenues — formal education, training programs, workshops, practical experience, and supervision. Mediators have the responsibility to constantly upgrade their skills and theoretical grounding, and shall endeavor to better themselves and the profession by seeking some form of further education in the negotiation and mediation process during each year in practice.

A mediator should promote the profession and make contributions to the field by encouraging and participating in research, publishing, or other forms of professional and public education.

Expertise

Mediators should perform their services only in those areas of mediation in which they are qualified either by experience or by training. Mediators should not attempt to mediate in an unfamiliar field or when there is risk of psychological, financial, legal, or physical damage to one of the parties due to the mediator's lack of experience.

A mediator is obligated to seek a co-mediator trained in the necessary discipline or refer cases to other mediators who are trained in the required field of expertise when he or she does not possess the required skills.

Voluntary Services

A mediator is obligated to perform some voluntary service during each year of practice to provide assistance to those who cannot afford to pay for mediation and to promote the field. It is left to the individual mediator to determine the amount and kind of service to be rendered for the good of the profession and of society.

Mediators should cooperate with their own and other agencies in establishing and maintaining the quality, qualifications, and standards of the profession. Mediators should participate in individual and agency evaluations, and should be supervised either by an agency, a mutually established peer, or the professional organization's board of ethics. Mediators involved in any breach of this code of conduct should notify their agency of the breach. Mediators hearing of violations of this code of ethics should also report this information to their agency or the board of ethics.

5. Responsibility of the Mediator to the Public and Other Unrepresented Parties

Negotiation is in essence a private, voluntary process. The primary purpose of mediation is to assist the parties in achieving a settlement. Such assistance does not abrogate the rights of the parties to resort to economic, social, psychological, and legal sanctions. However, the mediation process may include a responsibility of the mediator to assert the interest of the public or other unrepresented parties in order that a particular dispute be resolved, that costs or damages be alleviated, and that normal life be resumed. Mediators should question agreements that are not in the interest of the public or other unrepresented parties whose interests and needs should be and are not being considered. Mediators should question whether other parties' interests or the parties themselves should be present at negotiations. It is understood, however, that the mediator does not regulate or control any of the content of a negotiated agreement.

A mediator shall not use publicity to enhance his or her own position. When two or more mediators are mediating a dispute, public information should be managed by a mutually agreeable procedure.

APPENDIX C

Mediator Standards
**Report of the Ad Hoc Committee
Comprised of the Colorado Bar Association's
ADR Committee
and the Colorado Council
of Mediators and Mediation Organizations**

PART I: RECOMMENDED GUIDELINES FOR MEDIATOR
EDUCATION AND TRAINING

From the beginning of this project [completed in September 1992], we recognized we had a two-fold mission: to assist mediators in their pursuit of appropriate education and training, and to assist consumers, attorneys, judges and other professionals in selecting mediators. We propose the following recommendations be adopted as Guidelines for Mediator Education and Training in the areas of divorce and child custody disputes, as well as general civil disputes.

A principle which applies to all proposed guidelines is that it is the obligation of mediators to stay current on the pertinent substantive and procedural developments in the field. Consequently, each mediator should decide for himself or herself what training or education beyond these guidelines is needed. Additionally, the Committee recognizes that some mediators accept cases for limited purposes, acknowledging they are qualified to mediate fewer than all issues in a dispute. Those mediators should clearly disclose that information and act accordingly in accepting and facilitating disputes by either carefully limiting the issues to be mediated with him or her or by co-mediating with someone qualified in the other areas at issue.

With respect to the models set forth below, we found that the training requirements of the Academy of Family Mediators (AFM) served as a good model. We utilized the following eight "core" groups of skills and talents identified by the AFM as crucial elements to be considered:

1. Information Gathering Skills and Knowledge
(This core area must include a structured role-play dealing with a specific mediation scenario.)

    a.clients

        i.performing intake

        ii.screening clients

        iii.performing a needs assessment

        iv.contracting for services

    b.issues

        i.questioning

        ii.setting the agenda and prioritizing areas

        iii.identifying issues

        iv.screening clients

        v.exploring client interests and concerns

2. Relationship Skills and Knowledge

    a.forming relationships and building rapport

    b.establishing trust

    c.setting a cooperative tone

    d.establishing neutrality and impartiality

    e.empathetic listening and questioning

    f.empowering parties

    g.using self as a barometer for understanding client reactions

    h.staying non-judgmental

3. Communication Skills and Knowledge

    a.listening

    b.responding

c.guiding

d.paraphrasing

e.confronting

f.reframing

g.attending to non-verbal communication

h.identifying areas of consensus and disagreement

i.questioning

j.clarifying

k.using clear, neutral language

l.balancing communication

m.modeling constructive behavior

4. Problem-Solving Skills and Knowledge

(This core area must include a structured role-play dealing with a specific mediation scenario.)

a.identifying and analyzing problems and needs (also in #1)

b.collecting data (also in #1)

c.prioritizing issues (also in #1)

d.framing issues

e.narrowing issues

f.converting positions into needs and interests

g.educating clients

h.identifying areas of agreement

i.identifying principles and criteria to assist decision-making

j.designing temporary plans

k.developing options and brainstorming

l.evaluating options and consequences

m.testing reality

n.developing an implementation plan

o.assisting parties to identify alternatives to a mediated agreement

5. Ethical Decision-Making and Values, Skills, and Knowledge

a.understanding Academy and other mediation standards of ethical practice

b.being sensitive to parties' values, including culture

c.being non-judgmental

d.establishing a commitment to honest disclosure

e.maintaining dignified behavior

f.being respectful of the parties

g.not imposing personal and professional values

h.establishing and maintaining a right to self-determination by the parties

i.honoring the uniqueness of clients

j.ensuring individual responsibility of parties for themselves

k.establishing the importance of each individual's participation

l.ensuring voluntary agreements and participation

m.recognizing responsibilities to non-present parties

n.dealing with commonly encountered ethical dilemmas

6. Interaction and Conflict Management Skills and Knowledge

(This core area must include a structured role-play dealing with a specific mediation scenario.)

a.using ground rules

b.reducing tensions

c.balancing power

d.refocusing

e.confronting

f.strategizing/orchestrating

g.caucusing

h.managing impasse

i.empowering parties

j.distracting/redirecting

k.dealing with strong emotions

l.maintaining control of the process

m.managing the influence of outside parties

7. Professional Skills and Knowledge

a.contracting for services (also in #1)

b.case management

c.referring cases

d.community and legal resources

e.drafting memoranda

f.working with experts

g.obtaining, recording and monitoring factual information

h.dealing with complex factual material

i.conciliation, mediation, arbitration definitions and distinctions

8. Substantive Knowledge Base

(Introduction to Conflict Resolution Theory, Family Systems and Development, Domestic Violence Issues and Legal Context)

a.prevalent conflict resolution theories

b.basic concepts of family systems/dynamics

c.negotiation theory

d.mediation process

e.family violence

f.family life cycle

g.legal context

h.conciliation, mediation, arbitration definitions and distinctions
   (also in #7)

i.relevant sociological theories

j.relevant personality, communication and psychological theories

k.research on mediation effectiveness

Divorce and Child Custody Mediation

Because of alternative methods by which one can obtain or demonstrate the skills and talents identified above, we propose that divorce and child custody mediators follow the education and training guidelines in either Model Alternative A or B. All references to numbers of hours are to "clock" hours and not to credit hours.

Model Alternative A

1) A 40-hour divorce and child custody mediation training program which covers the eight components described above and includes at least six hours of role playing.

2) One hundred hours of mediation experience (solo or co-mediation) in at least 10 different cases while in consultation with an experienced mediator. One should participate in at least 15 hours of consultation. (An explanation of consultation is given at the end of this section.)

3) At least 12 additional hours of education in substantive areas of knowledge relevant to divorce and child custody mediation.

4) Subscription to a code of ethics or code of professional conduct for mediators that is sanctioned by a recognized professional organization.

5) Active participation in continuing education in the mediation process and in substantive areas. Continuing education can include, but is not limited to, information or knowledge gained through workshops, reading, peer consultation, video or audio tape review and lecture.

An Explanation of Consultation

1. Definition of consultation.

Consultation is a process in which a mediator presents, discusses and analyzes a mediation case with one or more other mediators. This involves examining both the process of the mediation and the substantive issues. The consultant's role is to help the mediator examine the case, conceptualize the issues and process, and offer support, advice and information. Consultation is not supervision and the consultant does not assume responsibility for the case. However, supervision satisfies the objectives and criteria of consultation.

2. Types of consultation.

A. Individual consultation. Individual consultation involves consultation with an experienced mediator, preferably one who has the education and training described in these guidelines.

B. Group consultation. Some consultation can occur in a group setting which includes an experienced mediator, as such education and training is described in these guidelines.

1) Family mediation: For Model Alternative A criteria, there should be a minimum of five hours of individual consultation. Every two hours of group consultation may be exchanged for one hour of individual consultation, so long as there are at least the five hours of individual consultation. For Model Alternative B criteria, there should be a minimum of three hours of individual consultation. The remaining hours may be met with either group consultation (two for one exchange) or individual consultation.

2) Civil mediation: Five hours of consultation are recommended. At least three hours should involve individual consultation. Every two hours of group consultation may be exchanged for one hour of individual consultation up to a total of two hours.

C.Co-mediation. When a mediator is either co-mediating or being directly observed by an educated and trained mediator, then every hour or portion of an hour of consultation after a session shall equal twice the time for consultation. For example, if a mediator co-mediates with an educated and trained mediator for a two-hour session, and then consults with the educated and trained co-mediator for half an hour, this shall count for one hour of consultation.

3.Documentation

Mediators are encouraged to document their education, training and consultation. It is understood that having documented consultation from an educated and trained mediator may be more difficult for mediators who are already in practice when these guidelines are adopted.

4.Confidentiality

The mediator, the consultant and the participants in any mediation consultation group shall adhere to any assurances of confidentiality provided to the parties, whether by law, ethical canon or agreement.

Model Alternative B

1) A 40-hour general or divorce and child custody mediation training program which covers the eight components described above and includes at least six hours of role playing.

2) A law degree or graduate degree in one of the behavioral sciences.

3) At least two years of professional experience working with people who are dealing with divorce and child custody related issues.

4) If the mediation training program was a general one, supplemental education in those substantive areas of knowledge which complement one's areas of experience. The possible areas include: the needs of children at different developmental stages; the emotional process of divorce; divorce statutes and case law; the division of property; and issues of child and spousal support.

5) Sixty hours of mediation experience (solo or co-mediation) in at least six different cases while in consultation with an experienced mediator. One should participate in at least eight hours of consultation.

6) Subscription to a code of ethics or code of professional conduct for mediators that is sanctioned by a recognized professional organization.

7) Active participation in continuing education in the mediation process and the substantive areas. Continuing education can include,

but is not limited to, information or knowledge gained through workshops, reading, peer consultation, video or audiotape review, and lecture.

Civil and Community Mediation

The range of mediated disputes is enormous, reflecting everything from business and labor/management to environment and insurance-related disputes, and everything in between. Accordingly, any model needs to recognize several givens:

– In certain areas, notably the resolution of labor/management disputes, mediators have served with distinction for many years without any formal requirements in terms of education and training or substantive expertise. While listing agencies may have established their own guidelines, it has been and continues to be the market which determines who is qualified.

– In a civil or community setting, it is frequently the case that mediators serve in a broad range of disputes. This presupposes either an enormous knowledge base or, more likely, a skills base which allows the mediator to utilize relevant substantive knowledge gained during the course of mediation.

Model

1) A 21-hour comprehensive mediator training program which covers the first seven skill components described above and includes at least six hours of role playing.

2) Thirty hours of mediation experience (solo or co-mediation) in at least 10 different cases while in consultation with an experienced mediator. One should participate in at least five hours of consultation.

3) Subscription to a code of ethics or code of professional conduct for mediators that is sanctioned by a recognized professional organization.

4) Active participation in continuing education in the mediation process and in substantive areas.

PART II: HISTORY OF PROJECT

In the fall of 1990, the Colorado Bar Association's Alternative Dispute Resolution Committee and the Colorado Council of Mediators and Mediation Organizations (CCMO) agreed to undertake a study of, and to report on, mediator qualifications as a joint committee project (the Committee). The Committee members all believe that the success of mediation depends on having trained and experienced mediators, but realize there is a wide difference of opinion as to qualifications and whether there should be voluntary adherence to those recommendations or whether there should be mandatory adherence. No one believed the task would be easy, and that belief has proven true.

The ultimate purpose in establishing education and training guidelines for any professional field is to protect the consuming public through assurance of a minimum level of competency. An important dilemma is how to do so without unnecessarily or inappropriately restricting access to a process and profession which are constantly and rapidly changing. These guidelines for education and training are intended as a set of standards for mediators to work toward as opposed to barriers that unnecessarily limit who can practice in this field. We believe that CCMO and those mediators who already meet these guidelines have an obligation to assist others by providing assistance in fulfilling these standards, especially the experience and consultation recommendations. This can be in various forms ranging from a single opportunity such as a consultation or participation as a co-mediator to a comprehensive internship program. These should be available in ways which are not cost prohibitive, including some low-cost or no-cost opportunities.

We issued a preliminary report in November 1991 and obtained comments and input to that report at a public meeting in early December 1991. We then presented a revised draft report to the ADR Committee and the CCMO membership in Spring 1992, and again solicited and considered suggestions for revisions.

At the recommendation of the CBA-ADR Committee, we asked for comments and suggestions from the Bar Association. After reviewing our request, reservations were expressed regarding language suggesting "qualifications." These concerns underscored the previous thinking of the Committee that its recommendations should not be perceived as limitations to participation in the process, but rather as "guidance" for aspiring mediators and consumers of mediation services. During subsequent Committee discussions, consensus was reached that the essence of the Committee's work was to provide guidelines for mediator education and training, whose focus is now reflected in this report. It should be understood that the Committee's recommendations are guidelines, and that there are "qualified" mediators who will not meet such recommendations, just as meeting the recommendations does not guarantee mediator competence.

PART III: EXISTING STATUTORY DEFINITION OF MEDIATION

Mediation is currently defined in § 13-22-302(2.4) of the Colorado Dispute Resolution Act as "an intervention in dispute negotiations by a trained neutral third party with the purpose of assisting the parties to reach their own decisions."

A "mediator" is defined in the Dispute Resolution Act as "a trained individual who assists disputants to reach a mutually acceptable resolution of their disputes by identifying and evaluating alternatives." C.R.S., § 13-22-302(4). There is no discussion of what the training consists of nor of the skills and knowledge base necessary to serve as a mediator.

PART IV: OUTLINE OF COMMITTEE ACTIVITIES TO DATE AND OF NECESSARY FUTURE ACTIVITIES

The Committee began its work by reviewing and discussing the report of the Society for Professionals in Dispute Resolution (SPIDR) Commission on Qualifications, numerous law review and other professional publication articles, a survey of other states' statutes regarding training, experience and qualifications, and reports from other states' alternative dispute resolution programs. The purpose of this investigatory work was to attempt to avoid duplication and to glean ideas which could be used as a basis for the Committee's work.

One important debate in mediation circles has been between credential-based qualifications and competency-based qualifications. While this can well apply to other professions, it is heightened for mediation due to people entering the unlicensed mediation profession with a variety of backgrounds and experiences. Some come with formal education, training and experience in other professions such as law, mental health, accounting, business and academia. There are also skilled mediators who are lay members of the community, who have a variety of levels of formal education and experience.

In the ideal world, if we had a good system for measuring competence, that is all that would be needed for determining who is a satisfactorily educated, trained and experienced mediator. Since that is not presently available, although there is an effort on the national level to develop such a system, the next best approach seems to be to base guidelines on the education, training, skills, knowledge and experience that are essential to be minimally competent as a mediator.

As a starting point, the Committee developed a template or grid to use for discussion purposes, which had along one dimension, possible uses of any recommendations, ranging from the least restrictive (public education of what qualifications a mediator should have) to the most restrictive (licensure). The qualifying elements of possible education, training and experience guidelines were listed along the second dimension, so that a cross-referencing and cross-focus could develop. The template was developed as a tool for discussion and brainstorming, and we made efforts not to evaluate ideas before fully discussing them.

Eventually, because of the enormous task of addressing possible licensure and certification practicalities, lack of an institutional structure for implementation and because of wide disagreement about the wisdom of having state regulations at these early stages of ADR, we decided to temporarily table those possibilities. Despite our differences, we agreed it would not be feasible to implement a mandatory statewide registration, certification or licensure program in the near future. Consequently, the Committee's work began to focus on the three least restrictive methods of quality control: public education, voluntary adherence and trade group adoption.

We agreed that certain skills and talents apply to all types or areas of mediation, such as information gathering, communication and interaction, and conflict-management skills. We also concluded that different types of disputes may require different levels or depths of substantive knowledge for effective mediation. For example, a mediator facilitating a dispute between a couple seeking a divorce may need knowledge about dissolution of marriage issues, whereas a mediator facilitating a dispute between a lender and a borrower may need knowledge about contract and collection issues.

The Committee remains divided, however, as to whether and to what degree a certain level of substantive knowledge should be obtained. Two basic concerns raised are: 1) that the mediator have enough substantive knowledge to provide meaningful assistance to the parties and 2) fear that good mediators could be unnecessarily or arbitrarily excluded if a high level of substantive knowledge were required. Nevertheless, in order to effectively serve as a mediator in any type of dispute, the mediator has an obligation to acquire enough knowledge to understand the substance of the issues in dispute.

Submission of this report does not complete the work that needs to be done to assist in educating the public and mediators about mediation education, training and experience. We therefore recommend that a group be formed from the CBA-ADR Committee, CCMO and any other professional group which has an interest in expanding our work and implementing plans, to distribute this information. Before these guidelines are disseminated to consumers, they should include other information consumers need to know, including: the appropriate relationship between the mediator and the disputants, and/or the disputants' attorneys, whether the mediator has experience in the particular type of dispute, and whether the mediator adheres to a conciliation, interest-based bargaining, or some other procedural model for mediation

We hope to see a future committee develop consumer and educational tools, including booklets, directories, pamphlets, a speakers' bureau on mediation, and articles for publication in professional journals and more widely distributed newspapers, magazines and media.

**For more information on
mediation sources and training:**

Sam Leonard
c/o Leonard Institute
4741 E. Palm Canyon Dr., Suite C140
Palm Springs, CA 92264
1-800-995-1985
e-mail: sleonard@doitnow.com